DETAILING TIPS AND TECHNIQUES

MODEL RAILROAD HANDBOOK NO. 35

From  Magazine

Model Railroader

Compiled by Bob Hayden
Cover design by Lawrence Luser
Cover photograph by Earl Smallshaw

The material in this book first appeared as articles in **MODEL RAILROADER** magazine.

First printing, 1993. Second printing, 1994.

KALMBACH BOOKS

Track and lineside details

Improve your track with small, simple details

BY JORY TETZLAFF
PHOTOS BY THE AUTHOR

RECENTLY, while on one of my weekly railfan jaunts along the Chicago & North Western's Butler, Wis., yard trackage, I became aware of the multitude of right-of-way detailing that can easily be applied to a model railroad. What first captured my attention was a profuse sprouting of what I thought to be nothing more than weed growth. Down on all fours to get a better look, I discovered that what I saw was spilled grain that had sprouted (fig. 1). Notice how it's basically concentrated between the rails rather than on the outside. It seems creosoted ties, ballast, and a bit of diesel oil and grease provide a perfect growing medium.

Surprisingly, this was all happening on a heavily traveled main line and not the usual siding or spur. In real life it wouldn't be long before the track maintenance crews sprayed a chemical killer on this growth before it got out of control, but for our modeling purposes, such flora is just the ticket to highlight an otherwise stark, squeaky-clean model roadbed. Figure 1 shows my model vignette of a grain spill.

DETAILS GALORE

As I strolled down the line, I began to realize that little things like these can truly enhance model track. I noticed other types of spillage including gypsum and a maintenance product called Oil-Dry (used to absorb oil and grease). There were also wood chips, cement, and various dry commodities.

With heightened interest it didn't take long before I came across other things that would be missed by a casual glance down the right-of-way. Shown in fig. 2 is an air hose. Other debris I saw included brake pads, coupler knuckles, metal strapping, wire, paper and cardboard scraps, bent spikes, used fishplates, and a coupler pin or two. Such details can give a layout character and flair.

The real beauty of all this is that most of this detailing can be accomplished using things already tucked away in a scrap box. I've confined my detailing to station areas and junctions, with the idea of implying more detail than is actually present. This form of modeling, combined with weathered rail and track, is truly convincing.

Figure 3 shows typical tracks that are adjacent to a main line. Weed growth abounds, and there are reasons for this. One thing is the cost of removing it. Also, it doesn't pose a real fire hazard. Due to reduced train speeds on secondary tracks, there is little likelihood of sparks from hot brake shoes igniting the growth. Weeds are an easy detailing project. Many commercial texturing materials are available, along with rope fibers and yarn scraps. Figure 4 is a scene I've created with weeds, spillage, and other details.

RIGHTS-OF-WAY

Some details can be more easily detected once you understand why they are there. The detail shown to the left in fig. 5 can be used in great numbers and is easily scratchbuilt. It is a C&NW equipment vault that houses relays, transformers, and signal operating gear. Made of concrete, it has a heavy-gauge steel cover topped with a chain and padlock to prevent unauthorized entry. The C&NW vaults are about 36" in diameter and 30" high. Power and control wires run underground through a cable to a 7- or 8-foot-high wooden (or metal) post, then up to lineside transmission lines.

To make a vault, I lightly sand the end of a round no. 2 lead pencil to give it a slight curve and then paint the top silver to represent the sheet-metal cover (fig. 5). A line post and stranded wire cable complete the project.

Ballast, creosote, and diesel lube oil and grease drippings don't seem to deter Mother Nature's ability to make vegetation grow, as seen on this heavily traveled main line. Between and around the tracks are many ideas for detail modeling.

Fig. 1. Left: This greenery is the sprouts from grain spilled along the tracks. **Above:** The author modeled the sprouts with plaster sprinkled with ground foam.

Fig. 2. Common debris found along most railroad rights-of-way include brake shoe pads, old coupler knuckles, and air hoses.

Fig. 3. Left: Tracks adjacent to a main line usually have weed overgrowth, which is burned off if it becomes a nuisance. Banged-up steel drums, metal strapping, and paper scraps are also found around railroad property. **Fig. 4. Above:** The author has combined a number of details including a diesel fuel supply tank into this small yard service area.

YARDS AND SERVICE TRACKAGE

At best, model yards are still quite condensed, but with some detailing we can enhance and improve their appearance. Yards and service areas are neither as full of debris nor as dirty and grimy as you might think. Safety is an all-important part of railroading, and excess debris, whether equipment or just plain junk, pose a danger to men and machines. Probably the most common thing found in a yard is spillage of various commodities such as I've described.

Many small yards have simple locomotive-servicing facilities, including sand delivery apparatus and fuel storage tanks. Figure 6 shows a rack of m.u. connectors, a broom, and a storage shed. Around the tracks there's a lot of oil and grease and spilled sand.

SIGNS

Another scenic element I use is name signs. Figure 7 shows a model version of this detail on my layout. These signs are found at yards, junctions, and town and city limits among other places. Besides signs located along the mainline right-of-way, there are many in and around

Fig. 5. Left: Railroads use a large number of vaults to house electrical equipment for signaling and communication. This is a concrete one on the C&NW that's buried in the ground. Its sheet-metal cover is secured with a chain and padlock. **Above:** Here's the author's simplified HO model of the cable post and concrete vault.

yard and service areas. Typical ones are "stop," "no clearance," and "speed limit." Signs like these can be mounted on metal stakes, wooden posts, or on the sides of structures that are close to tracks.

It's awesome how much detail can be found on the prototype, and I've only scratched the surface. But maybe my bringing a few of these features to light will help you enhance your own layout. Do some railfanning, and snap pictures of things that attract your attention. Those photos will help in reproducing what you've seen. I'm sure you'll be impressed with how a little detailing can give your layout some flair. Best of all, you can add these details at your leisure while still having fun running trains. ◊

Fig. 6. Ideas for an endless number of detailing projects can be found around a real railroad yard engine facility. Visible in this scene at a small C&NW facility are locomotive m.u. connectors hung on a structural steel rack, a broom, sand, grease and oil spillage, and a storage container.

Fig. 7. The town limit sign in this model scene on the author's layout has a post made from a fireplace match stick and a stripwood and paper nameboard. This sign identifies a junction, but the author generally locates these signs a scale ¼ mile from the communities on his layout.

Above: The engine terminal on the author's layout has a wide array of junk scattered around it. Proper coloring is the key to making debris look effective. Metal parts, for example, are found in many shades of rust. **Fig. 1. Left:** The scrap box is an excellent source of junk. Every modeler has at least one such container filled with leftover kit parts, extra bits of wood and metal, castings, and bits and pieces of siding, plastic, and stripwood.

Modeling junk

Litter can liven up a layout's appearance

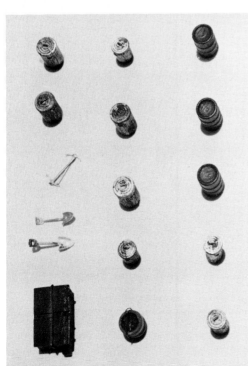

Fig. 2. Left: Detail parts and discarded or unused castings from various structure kits can be positioned around your layout individually or clustered together. This collection of parts includes several types of metal storage barrels and cans, along with a shovel and a pick. **Fig. 3. Above:** Another view of the yard area on the author's layout shows wood strips representing planks and timbers, different kinds of barrels, and gears all scattered among the weeds. There's even a saddle tank and boiler from an old steam locomotive kit.

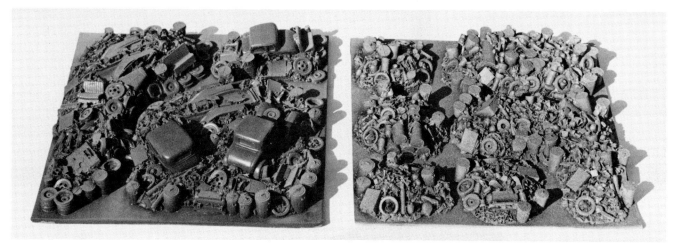

BY CARL CAIATI

DON'T LET the title mislead you into thinking this is a treatise on bad modeling. It's actually about one of the most common elements in our world, yet one that's often overlooked when model railroaders scenick their layouts. I'm talking about junk. Junk, or perhaps litter is a better term, is found everywhere: in backyards and construction sites, around garages and farms, really almost anywhere you look. And don't forget that universal institution, the junkyard. I don't know if we can say junk glorifies the scenic aspects of a model railroad, but it does add a novel and necessary touch of realism.

Junk is relatively easy to model. It need not be uniform or seem planned. Instead, it should be scattered, and the sloppier and more disoriented it is the more natural it appears. Generally junk or litter is composed of all types of materials. One exception is scrap metal destined for reclamation. That will be made up of similar metals, with no wood or foreign materials mixed in.

Raw materials for junk are easy for every modeler to come by. The obvious source is the scrap box. We all have one filled with parts set aside for some future use that seldom comes to pass. Included in most scrap boxes are ties, wood strips, pieces of tubing, car and structure kit parts, and various castings. Any of these can be put into piles or scattered indiscriminately around yards and along the right-of-way. Good coloring is essential for all junk. I use an airbrush and such Floquil weathering colors as Rust, Dust, and Grime.

You can also buy commercial junk castings, such as those that are made by Chooch and Woodland Scenics. These can be used as is, cut into smaller sections, or combined into a large junk pile featuring all sorts of scrap metal.

Whether you make your own or buy "ready-to-use" junk, the possibilities for applying it to your layout are endless. Look at where litter and debris are found on prototype railroads, or let your imagination run wild. Either way, adding a variety of such materials will make your model railroad look more realistic and give it the flair that appeals to visitors. ⧈

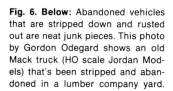

Fig. 4. In HO scale Chooch Enterprises offers junk pile modules that are cast in urethane. These can be assembled as a single large heap or cut apart to make smaller pieces.

Fig. 5. Right: Cast metal or plastic, or turned wooden barrels, may be drilled out and then filled with wood refuse (as is shown here) or other scrap materials. Wood barrels (not often seen in use these days) and metal drums are commonly found around railroad and industrial shops.

Fig. 6. Below: Abandoned vehicles that are stripped down and rusted out are neat junk pieces. This photo by Gordon Odegard shows an old Mack truck (HO scale Jordan Models) that's been stripped and abandoned in a lumber company yard.

Traffic around Hoosic Junction should increase, now that the author has finished this new highway. Lou, who photographed this scene on his HO layout, shares his secrets for constructing such realistic roads.

Follow the blacktop road

Painting sand is the secret to making realistic highways

BY LOU SASSI

THERE ARE many blacktop roads on my HO scale West Hoosic Division layout, but one consistently receives compliments from visitors. It meanders through the countryside around Hoosic Junction. As it turns out, this was one of the easiest and least expensive to make.

The road is sand. Yep, the same stuff you see at the beach. Although I get mine from fields near my home in upstate New York, you could use sandbox sand from a discount store or garden supply center. Whatever the source, just be sure there's no clay in your sand. Strain it first by pouring it through a fine-mesh kitchen sieve. The finer particles become road; what's left over can be saved for ground cover.

PAVEMENT LOCATION

Now that we've strained the sand, let's journey into the bush, so to speak, and prepare the road site. Using what Brad Short calls the "easyshell scenery" method (see the April 1987 MR), I start with a cardboard base covered with plaster gauze. After brushing brown latex paint on the gauze, I cover the paint liberally with sand, dyed sawdust, ground foam, and anything else that gives the look and texture of *real* ground cover.

I moisten this mess and apply a mixture of white glue and water to fix everything. Once that has dried, I vacuum up all loose ground cover.

ROAD BUILDING

Next, I cut cardboard strips the width of the pavement and lay them where the road will go. (The cardboard is the kind used for boxes at grocery stores.) Once the cardboard is in place, I spray the ground on either side with "wet" water (water mixed with a drop or two of liquid dishwashing detergent).

I take 3"-wide plaster gauze and cut it into strips that are 5" long. I dip these in water and lay them over the cardboard as shown in the drawing. Two layers of gauze ought to be enough to support the finished road.

Painting the gauze with the same earth color of latex comes next. Then I sprinkle on sand, trying to make the surface as smooth as possible. I spray this with wet water before using an eyedropper to apply a mixture of 3 parts water and 1 part white glue over everything.

PAINTING

To make sand the color of blacktop, I paint it with artist's acrylics. I use tubes of Hyplar paints from Grumbacher, though any brand should give the same results. While the road is drying, I mix Titanium White and Mars Black with water to achieve a medium shade of gray with the consistency of white glue. For a newer, smoother road, use a thicker mixture that has more black. For an older and rougher road, make it thinner and lighter in color. Experiment until you get the texture and color you want.

I squeeze out about 2" of each color and dilute it, then brush the mixture onto the road with a 1/2"-wide stiff-bristle artist's oil-color brush. Once the base color is down, I highlight each lane with random tones of lighter and darker gray in the direction of traffic. This gives the effect of spilled oil, grease, and discoloration from vehicles and weather.

STEP ONE

Apply highway-width cardboard to existing scenery base; spray edges with "wet" water

STEP TWO

Cover with two layers of wet plaster gauze

Let dry and paint

STEP THREE

Sprinkle with sand and secure with water/white glue mixture

STEP FOUR

Paint with artist's acrylics

After the acrylics have dried, I get out my ground foam, sawdust, and dirt and work the new ground cover up to the edge of the pavement. I again secure everything with my diluted white glue. Now the inhabitants of Hoosic Junction are able to travel more swiftly. I just hope the new highway doesn't take away too much passenger and freight traffic from the railroad. ☼

Scratchbuild a fleet

If you have water on your layout, rowboats are a natural

BY GARRY F. CERRONE

AS A YOUTH growing up along the Delaware River, I spent a lot of happy hours around boats and on the water. Pleasant memories of those days prompted me to include a waterfront scene on my layout.

Once again falling back on youthful experiences, I decided to build a few "for hire" styrene rowboats similar to a full-size plywood version that I built 20 years ago. Since this is a straightforward cut-and-paste project, I suggest you build more than one boat at a time. To build your own fleet you'll need .020" sheet styrene, Evergreen .010" x 6" styrene strips, solvent glue, and paint of your choice.

Begin by making patterns from the accompanying drawings and then cutting as many transoms and sides as you'll need. Begin assembly by gluing two sides to a transom. When this assembly can be handled, glue in seat supports made from strip styrene. While the transom seams are curing, fashion the rear, bow, and center seats from sheet stock. When the rear joints have set up, add the rear seat and let it dry. Now apply some solvent to both sides at the bow and carefully clamp the sides together with a spring clothespin. When this seam has dried, add the center and bow seats.

When all of the joints have cured, trace the outline of the bottom of the boat on a piece of sheet stock, cut it out, and glue this piece to the bottom. Trim this as necessary after the bottom seams have cured.

After you've added gunwales made from styrene stripping, your boats are ready for painting. I painted mine with Floquil Barrier and followed that with Floquil railroad colors.

Well, time to go fishing! ☼

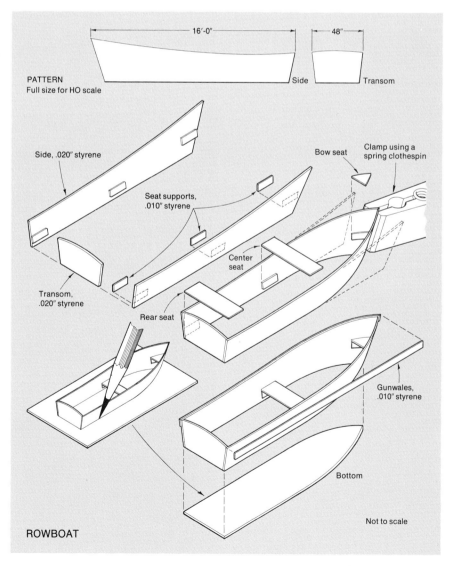

PATTERN
Full size for HO scale

16'-0" 48"

Side Transom

Side, .020" styrene

Seat supports, .010" styrene

Bow seat

Clamp using a spring clothespin

Center seat

Transom, .020" styrene

Rear seat

Gunwales, .010" styrene

Bottom

Not to scale

ROWBOAT

A view of some oil drums scattered around near a structure on the author's layout. The author used .005"-thick aluminum sheet for these barrels and embossed four raised bands on each form with a soft pencil. Various paint colors indicate different petroleum products contained inside each barrel.

Roll out the barrel

Make scale barrels or drums with aluminum sheet

BY MICHAEL TYLICK
PHOTOS BY THE AUTHOR

HERE'S a simple method of making realistic model steel drums that is especially suited to O and larger scales. The .005"-thick aluminum sheet material that I use is made by J. L. Hammett of Braintree, Mass., and is available at most art supply stores.

CONSTRUCTION

After determining the drums should be 24" in diameter and 36" high, I made a grooving die on linoleum with four properly spaced grooves. I place a sheet of aluminum on the die and emboss the four equally spaced welts with a soft pencil. Cut the sheet just outside the two end embossings, making it about ¾" high and 2" wide. See fig. 1.

Place the sheet on a soft cloth pad, with the welts down. With one ¾" edge parallel to a ½"-diameter dowel axis, roll the sheet into a cylinder. Unroll and wrap it again, this time starting with the last ¾" edge to be rolled. The first edge will now end up on top, on the outside of the drum form.

The "trained" curve will hold the overlapped ends tight together, and the seam will be almost invisible. Hide the seam by positioning the finished model against a structure wall or another drum, or lay the barrel on the ground, seam side down.

Next, make the top and bottom from .010"-thick styrene, cutting these pieces out with a draftsman's compass fitted with a circle cutting blade. See fig. 2. Slip these into the top and bottom grooves, and secure with a styrene cement (solvent). The scale 3"-diameter bungs, or filler caps, are made from .010"-thick styrene disks punched out with a leather hole punch.

PAINTING AND WEATHERING

Crumple, tear, or puncture some drums for variety. Spray with gray auto primer, and brush-paint them with Polly S or Tamiya paints. While black is a common oil drum color, many have one or two contrasting bright color bands. To finish the models, I apply emblem and logo decal pieces from Microscale HO gas station and oil drum cover signs. Three sheets are available: numbers 87-420, 87-421, and 87-422. Set the decals with Solvaset, and apply a few coats of Polly S Flat Finish to hide the decal film.

Weather the drums with washes of Polly S nos. 410003 Dust and 410073 Rust, along with India ink thinned with alcohol. I also applied some pastel chalk weathering, which I sealed with Grumbacher Tuffilm fixative.

I enjoy making detail parts in this manner. I save a few dollars, become a little less dependent on finding unusual detail items, and end up with unique pieces. The drum models go together so easily and quickly that I wouldn't be overwhelmed by making enough of them to model a chemical plant or tank farm. I've used the same corrugation embossing technique to make drainage pipe. And I've made a few spike cans that scale 12" in diameter and 18" high. These have a single roll at both the top and bottom. ◘

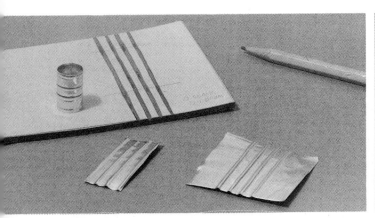

Fig. 1. The author's embossing die has cut correctly spaced grooves in a piece of linoleum. Next, using a soft pencil, four drum welts are embossed into .005"-thick aluminum sheet.

Fig. 2. Drum tops and bottoms, along with the bungs, are made from .010"-thick styrene and cemented in place with plastic cement. A few barrels can be dented and beat up for variety.

Boston & Maine 4-4-0 no. 934 crawls up to the ashpit at the Williamstown engine facilities on Lou Sassi's HO scale West Hoosic Division layout.

Ashes to ashes

Using real ashes to detail your steam locomotive ashpit

BY LOU SASSI
PHOTO BY THE AUTHOR

ONCE THE engine facilities had been completed in the town of Williamstown on my HO scale Boston & Maine West Hoosic Division, I decided to start detailing some of the scenes it included. One detail noticeably lacking was the presence of ashes in the steam locomotive ashpit. Then a visit to Frank Czubryt's HOn3 layout yielded the answer to my dilemma. Looking closely at his Chama Yard, I noticed some very realistic ashes in the locomotive ashpit. When asked what he used to create such amazingly authentic ashes, his answer was all too

apparent: *ashes!* In this case, cigar ashes, but ashes all the same.

Well if cigar ashes would work, why not some other kind? Not being a cigar smoker, I decided that fireplace ashes should achieve the same look. Unfortunately, I also had no fireplace, but had a neighbor who did. So off I strolled to his house with a small jar in hand. Once convinced that I had not lost my mind (or thinking it best just to humor me and get me out of his house as quickly as possible), he presented me with a heaping jar of fireplace ashes.

To make the ashes permanent, I used a light spray of wet water (water with a drop or two of dishwashing detergent added) and a few eyedroppers of 3:1 water and white glue mix to prepare the

area. The ashes were then sprinkled by hand onto the mix and allowed to dry.

Usually when doing water-base scenery, the white glue mix is added to the ground cover materials after they are applied. This doesn't work with ashes. If the glue is added after they're applied, it will cause them to dissipate through the glue mix and the whole mess dries flat and unrealistic, looking like a glob of white mud. Therefore, the ashes must be added to the glue mix. When done this way, they will be permanently attached but appear fluffy and loose.

I used a Bright Boy to clean the railheads next to the pit, trying not to disturb the finished ashes. They'll last for years and look good. That's it, from ashes to ashes. ✸

With telltales in place, HO scale brakemen on the Boston & Maine West Hoosic Div. don't have to fear being unwillingly removed from atop a train.

A tale of telltales

Using fence material to build realistic telltales

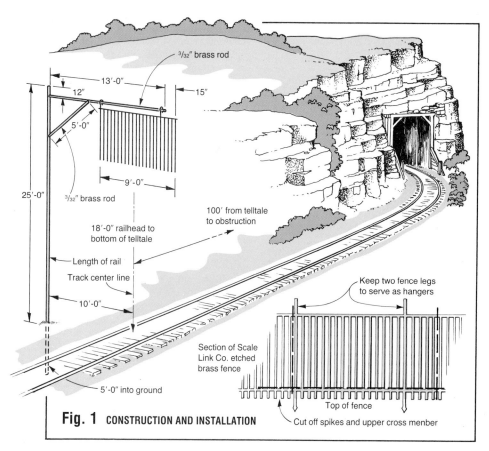

Fig. 1 CONSTRUCTION AND INSTALLATION

- ³/₃₂" brass rod
- 13'-0"
- 12"
- 15"
- 5'-0"
- 25'-0"
- ³/₃₂" brass rod
- 9'-0"
- 100' from telltale to obstruction
- 18'-0" railhead to bottom of telltale
- Length of rail
- Track center line
- 10'-0"
- 5'-0" into ground
- Keep two fence legs to serve as hangers
- Section of Scale Link Co. etched brass fence
- Top of fence
- Cut off spikes and upper cross member

BY LOU SASSI
PHOTOS BY THE AUTHOR

BACK IN the good ol' days of railroading (ask an old-time railroader, and he may argue about that description), when brakemen walked the roofs of their freight trains, telltales were installed at locations where overhead clearances were low enough to prematurely remove an unsuspecting individual from atop his mount. The telltale's ropes would brush against a trainman to warn him that it was time to duck. Highway overpasses, through bridges, and tunnels all necessitated such precautions. Although they varied somewhat from railroad to railroad, telltales were usually quite simple in their design.

DESIGN AND MATERIALS

Since my HO scale mid-1950s B&M West Hoosic Division includes a number of tunnels and bridges, I thought Philip R. Hasting's book *The Boston & Maine* would be a good place to look for a typical design used by that road. Sure enough, on page 162, Mogul no. 1402 was passing under a perfect example of a single-track telltale.

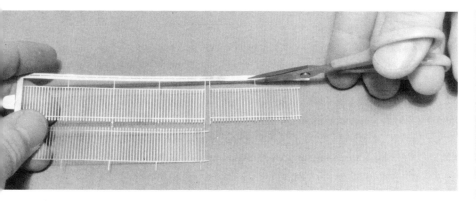

FIG. 2. TRIMMING THE FENCING
Above: Leave the fence legs intact when trimming the material. **Below:** Trim off the spikes at the top of the fence to form telltale ropes.

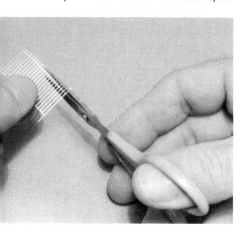

After studying the photo and approximating its scale, I came up with the dimensions shown in fig. 1. The B&M used rail for the post and what appears to be piping for the horizontal and diagonal members. I used code 55 rail (you could substitute code 70 or 83) for the post and $1/32''$ brass rod for the members.

The most difficult part of the project was finding something to represent the telltales themselves. The prototype used ropes or cables strung vertically from the horizontal member. While searching through my scrap box, I discovered some leftover etched-brass fencing from the Scale Link Co. (Scale Link Centre, 54 Church St., Twickenham, TW1 3NR, England). By cutting off the upper horizontal cross member and the spikes of the individual posts (fig. 2) and leaving the former fence legs as hangers, I could quickly turn a nine-scale-foot length of fence into a string of 21 telltale cables. It's necessary to retain at least two fence legs per telltale to use as hangers.

CONSTRUCTION AND PAINTING

Since I needed a batch (nine to be exact) of these little devils, I decided that mass production was the best way to approach the project. Once the telltales were trimmed and set aside, I began construction of the supporting structures.

I first cut 30-foot lengths of rail and then 13- and 5-foot lengths of rod with a cutoff disk in my Dremel Moto-Tool (you can also use a razor saw). To make soldering easier, I spiked each assembly to a makeshift jig on a scrap of 1 x 2 pine. After placing some flux at the joints with a toothpick, everything was soldered together (fig. 3).

I removed the spikes and, while care-

FIG. 3. SOLDERING
Spike the parts to a piece of pine to hold them in place for soldering the telltale assembly.

fully holding the completed assemblies in one hand, bent the telltale hangers (the former legs of the fence) around the horizontal pipes. A drop of five-minute epoxy at the end of these pipes keeps the telltales from sliding off.

Once the telltales were attached, everything was washed in a bath of denatured alcohol, then airbrushed Floquil Grimy Black. After the paint had dried for a day, I drybrushed on some raw sienna tube acrylic paint to create a rusty look. The telltales were ready to install.

You'll notice that Scale Link Co. is located in England. Don't let this deter you from ordering the fencing. The price for spear point railings (item no. F29 G. W. R.) is £3.95, which is about $7 American. One batch of fence material will yield 12 telltales. The easiest way to order is to send your VISA or Master-Card number with your order. Scale Link will bill your credit card for the material and postage costs. You can also obtain an international money order from your post office. ⚙

Inexpensive O scale vehicles

Modified and weathered toys can look great on your layout

BY MICHAEL TYLICK
PHOTOS BY THE AUTHOR

MY WIFE JANET is sure smart. She wanted to add a family room to our house, and she convinced me by agreeing to a basement underneath. Soon I'll have a new large train room, and I'm considering switching from HO to O scale traction. In the meantime, I've been looking around to see what's available. At a recent train show, Dave Newcomb told me about Matchbox's "Models of Yesteryear" vehicles, many of which are suitable for O once they've been toned down and weathered. As this article will show, they're also good grist for the kitbasher's mill.

THE WOODIE

Figure 1 shows the original toy Ford delivery truck that I kitbashed into a vintage station wagon. At a proportion of 1:40, it's a bit large for O scale (1:48) but still quite usable. These delivery trucks retail for about $7, maybe $5 in a discount toy store, but I found some on sale for $2.50 and stocked up.

To make the woodie I first disassembled the Ford by grinding off the rivet ends with a motor tool. I made the model look a little smaller by lowering and flattening the roof. Doing so made the hood look too tall, so I shaved 1/32" off its bottom.

For the driver I used an inexpensive K-Line figure, cutting off the legs at the hips and knees and then gluing them back so the little fellow could sit down. I also repositioned his left arm to hold the steering wheel. Filler putty smoothed up the joints quite well.

While I've found working with HO figures to be very tedious, it's simple and fun in the larger size. I've also found that washes of contrasting watercolors settle into the cracks and folds and really help to bring out the details.

Next, I brushed on a coat of Polly S Flat Finish to provide a base for further painting, which was also done with Polly S. These water-base paints are nontoxic and work very well for small painting projects in which many colors are needed. I think many people would like this paint once they had tried it. I painted the hood with a dull yellow mixed from Reefer Yellow, Concrete, and Reefer White.

To represent the wood body I brushed on a base coat of Mud, let it dry, then stippled it with burnt umber watercolor. I gave the raised trim a second coat to darken it, adding a little rubbing alcohol to the water to make the trim paint more opaque. This gave a pretty good simulation of the maple wood sides of the real car. After painting the dashboard and seats, I sealed everything with a coat of Testor's Dullcote.

I didn't want to weather the woodie too much, so applied a wash of India ink and alcohol to bring out the detail and add a little road grime. Some yellow ochre and dark gray pastel chalks were dusted on to blend everything together and add a little age. I've found it necessary to apply a coat of Grumbacher Matte Tuffilm Fixative over pastels before spraying on Dullcote, which seems to erase the chalk.

For a nice final touch I typeset a license plate on a computer (Commodore 64 using GEOS), first making it oversize and then reducing it on a copy machine.

FORD COAL TRUCK

Another of my Ford automobiles went under the knife and became the coal truck shown in fig. 2. After total disassembly

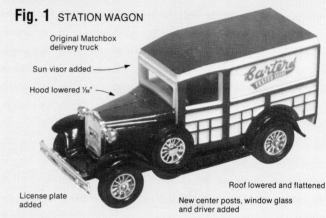

Fig. 1 STATION WAGON

Original Matchbox delivery truck
Sun visor added
Hood lowered 1/32"
Roof lowered and flattened
License plate added
New center posts, window glass and driver added

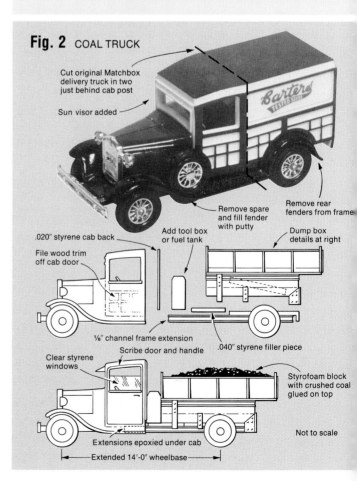

Fig. 2 COAL TRUCK

Cut original Matchbox delivery truck in two just behind cab post
Sun visor added
Remove spare and fill fender with putty
Remove rear fenders from frame
Add tool box or fuel tank
Dump box details at right
.020" styrene cab back
File wood trim off cab door
1/8" channel frame extension
.040" styrene filler piece
Scribe door and handle
Clear styrene windows
Styrofoam block with crushed coal glued on top
Extensions epoxied under cab
Extended 14'-0" wheelbase
Not to scale

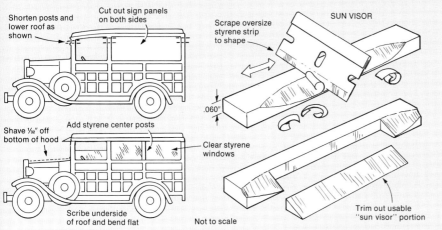

Shorten posts and lower roof as shown

Cut out sign panels on both sides

SUN VISOR

Scrape oversize styrene strip to shape

.060"

Add styrene center posts

Clear styrene windows

Shave 1/2" off bottom of hood

Scribe underside of roof and bend flat

Not to scale

Trim out usable "sun visor" portion

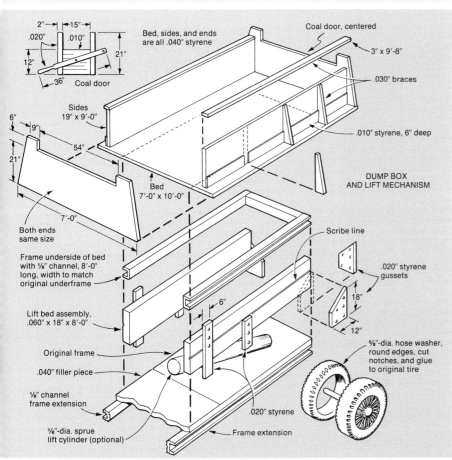

2" 15"

.020" .010"

12" 21"

36" Coal door

Bed, sides, and ends are all .040" styrene

Coal door, centered

3" x 9'-8"

.030" braces

.010" styrene, 6" deep

DUMP BOX AND LIFT MECHANISM

Sides 19" x 9'-0"

6" 9"

54"

21"

7'-0"

Both ends same size

Frame underside of bed with 1/8" channel, 8'-0" long, width to match original underframe

Lift bed assembly, .060" x 18" x 8'-0"

Original frame

.040" filler piece

1/8" channel frame extension

1/8"-dia. sprue lift cylinder (optional)

Frame extension

Bed 7'-0" x 10'-0"

Scribe line

.020" styrene gussets

18"

12"

6"

5/8"-dia. hose washer, round edges, cut notches, and glue to original tire

.020" styrene

I filed off the woodie boards with a large flat file; then I smoothed the sides with an X-acto chisel blade. I patched the nicks with body putty, smoothed them with an emery board, and then built a back for the cab. A dental pick made an excellent scriber for the new door and door handles.

Using a hacksaw I cut the frame in two just behind the cab. The rear fenders were removed and saved for some future junk pile. With epoxy I attached a 1/8" Plastruct channel under the frame to extend the wheelbase to a scale 14 feet.

I built a dump body for the truck from styrene. This work went very fast using methyl ethyl ketone (MEK), which bonds the plastic almost immediately. Styrene is great for models of metal prototypes. It's very strong, scale thickness can be used, and the texture is very similar to that of metal.

Somewhere I miscalculated and the cab and body came out too far apart. I fudged my way out by adding a small box to fill the gap. This might contain tools or fuel, but whatever it does it solved my problem.

The truck just didn't look right without dual rear wheels to hold the weight of the coal. To represent the inside tires I used hose washers that very fortunately were just the right size. After securing the washer tires to the model with epoxy, I rounded the washer edges with a hobby knife and carved in some semblance of tread. To accommodate the extra wheel width, I had to cut the axle in half with a motor tool. A lump of putty filled the gap by representing a differential housing.

I don't think too many coal trucks were very clean, so I had fun weathering this one. Before starting, though, I cut a semicircular piece of masking tape (using a knife blade in a compass) to place on the windshield and keep the wiper area clean. Then I applied washes of Mud and Dirt, followed by some India ink and alcohol grime. I used earth tone chalks for "splashed mud" along the bottom and black chalk for coal dust around the body. Warm, light gray pastels blended it all together. After a coat of sealer, a coat of Dust melded everything into an old-looking vehicle. I finished with some streaks of Rust around the frame and coal door.

The coal load is a carved chunk of Styrofoam painted with India ink. To represent coal I smashed some real coal with a hammer and sifted out the larger chunks. I painted white glue on the Styrofoam and sprinkled on coal, followed by an eyedropper full of diluted white glue. The coal load took several days to dry.

Since becoming interested in these models I've been looking more closely in toy stores for useful pieces. My interest is in O, but I've noticed other toy lines that should be useful in other scales. Among them are Ertl, which makes 1:64 (S) models, and Matchbox, whose vehicles are about right for HO. The economics of mass production makes these toys inexpensive, and with many you'd only have to do some toning down and repainting to prepare them for your layout. ⚙

Superdetailing HO automobiles

Etched detail parts turn nice models into stunning miniatures

BY HENRIK PRAETORIUS
PHOTOS BY THE AUTHOR

IT REALLY is a small world. I live in Denmark, and my HO railroad features Swiss railroading from 1950 to 1960. The Swiss favored American-built automobiles more than most other European countries did, so I wanted some nice American car models. Another reason was that when these cars began arriving in Europe just after the war they made a great impression on me and my friends, who had been virtually without autos of any kind for several years.

Unfortunately, most of the nice HO automobiles offered today are made in Germany, and most of the prototypes are European. A good number of the American cars I spotted in the Walthers catalog were from Alloy Forms. When I started to build some of these I found that the detailing was not as good as I would like. To improve them I started making etched replacement parts, especially window frames and grills.

In every case I had to find suitable photos to help with details, but it's surprising what you can find when you are really looking for it. My best sources are old magazines and magazines for car collectors.

Here are some typical etched parts by the author. Polished nickel silver represents chrome-plated parts very effectively. Detail relief is easy when etching from both sides.

Far left: Our author is modeling Switzerland, but many of the automobiles are American. All have been modified and superdetailed by adding etched nickel-silver parts. The Alloy Forms '57 Chevy, left, sports a new top and grill. The '46 Plymouth, center, was built from an Alloy Forms kit for a '41 Plymouth. Right is a '38 Ford made from a Jordan kit for a '39 model. **Left:** A Buick convertible with continental spare tire kit would have created a sensation anywhere, so no wonder the Swiss mechanic working on the '46 Plymouth is impressed. The Buick's windshield, sunshades, and rear-view mirror are a single etching. **Above:** The sporty red convertible is an Alloy Forms '48 Ford equipped with a photoetched windshield, side windows, and other details. The top cover is made from the lead foil used to seal champagne bottles. The green car behind the convertible may look American, but it's a 1951 German-built Opel Kapitän.

Below: Now here's a civilized way to wait for a train — an outdoor table on a sunny day! In the center is an Alloy Forms '41 Plymouth coupe.

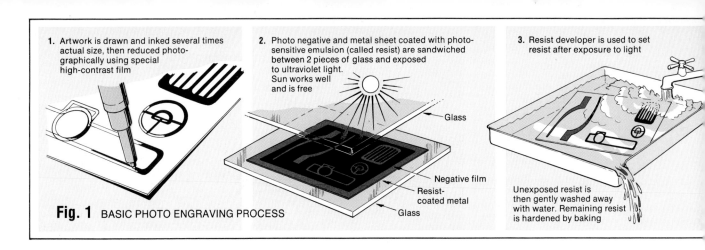

1. Artwork is drawn and inked several times actual size, then reduced photographically using special high-contrast film

2. Photo negative and metal sheet coated with photosensitive emulsion (called resist) are sandwiched between 2 pieces of glass and exposed to ultraviolet light. Sun works well and is free

Glass

Negative film

Resist-coated metal

Glass

3. Resist developer is used to set resist after exposure to light

Unexposed resist is then gently washed away with water. Remaining resist is hardened by baking

Fig. 1 BASIC PHOTO ENGRAVING PROCESS

FIG. 2. SUPERDETAILING A BUICK

Above: Here's an out-of-the-box Revell-Praline Buick. **Right:** After studying catalogs and magazines our author prepares artwork that's three times actual size for etching detail parts. **Below:** Here are some of the etched parts. For convertibles the windshield and side window trim are all one piece. **Bottom:** Here are two shots of the finished sedan. The etched side trim pieces and portholes are particularly effective.

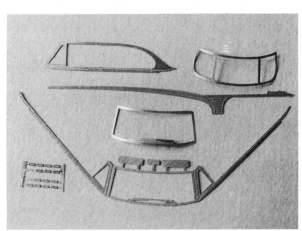

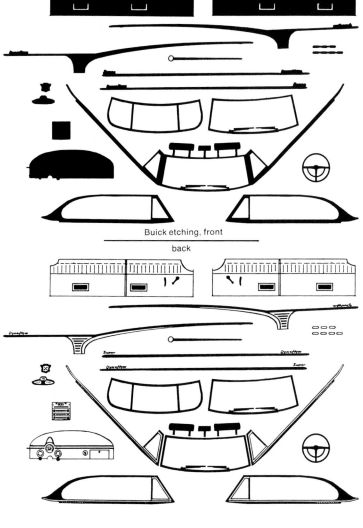

Buick etching, front

back

4. Acid bath dissolves the metal that is unprotected by the resist, yielding desired parts

Wear protective gloves and be careful when handling any acids

FIG. 3: A RAGTOP VERSION
Above: Another plastic Buick yielded this convertible. Note that the side trim is different from that for the sedan shown in fig. 2. **Below:** The top has been removed, and that bulky steering wheel will soon follow. The etched windshield is ready to be cemented in place. **Bottom:** The etched steering wheel and dashboard really dress up the car's interior.

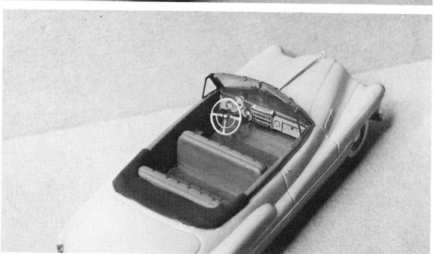

PHOTOETCHING INFORMATION AND SUPPLIES

Modelers interested in photo-etching can contact a KTI Chemicals distributor for more information and materials. (These are the products formerly offered by Kodak.) One distributor that handles small orders is PC&E, 522 Rt. 30, Frazer, PA 19355; phone 215-296-8585.

Automobile Arts (a British firm) has an etching kit — contact In Scale Hobby Supply, 701 Broad St. Menasha, WI 54952. A source for nickel silver is Craftsman Specialty Supply, 6608 Forty Mile Rd., Rogers City, MI 49779.

A helpful article is Wayne Wesolowski's "Chemical Milling," which is in the NMRA *Bulletin* for November 1986. Copies may be obtained for $1.50 each from the National Model Railroad Association, Headquarters Office, 4121 Cromwell Rd., Chattanooga, TN 37421.

Also very useful is John Stenbakken's article "Scratchparts by photoetching" in the September 1970 MR. Copies are available for $2.95, plus $1.50 postage and handling from Kalmbach Publishing Co., P. O. Box 1612, Waukesha, WI 53187-1612. ⓞ

DRAWINGS AND ETCHINGS

The first step in making these parts was to draw them three times actual size, taking care they came as close as possible to the original but still fit the model. See fig. 1. I always made two drawings, one for the parts as seen from the front, another from the rear. By etching from both sides at once I was able to add detail and relief.

Then from the drawings I made photo negatives, using an old enlarging apparatus as a camera. Then I made the etchings using a process similar to that used in making printed-circuit boards, except that I used .015″ nickel silver instead of printed-circuit-board material. Going into the process here would become too involved.

Figure 2 shows the steps I took in superdetailing a Revell-Praline Buick.

Shown in fig. 3 is a convertible made using the same techniques. These happen to be plastic models, but the principles are the same as for cast-metal models like those offered by Alloy Forms.

Installing the parts takes a lot of careful filing and double-checking. But even though these improvements are time consuming, I find the results worth the effort. Today I have a nice collection of unique models. ⓞ

Weathering figures

A simple technique that makes scale figures fit right in

BY RICHARD AND BILL GARDNER
PHOTOS BY THE AUTHORS

EVER SINCE John Allen put pigeons and their droppings on his prize-winning enginehouse, model railroaders have been spending a great deal of talent and energy weathering elements of their layout. Structures, vehicles, and rolling stock are natural candidates for weathering. All are elements that come together to create the scene.

But we have long overlooked one important element of the scene — the scale model figure. Having little people on the layout or diorama gives it a sense of scale, identifies the type of activity modeled, helps establish the time period, and contributes to the overall realism.

Our model figures accomplish some of these requirements right off the dealer's shelf; however, the level of realism we achieve in the rest of our modeling generally isn't attained when it comes to figures. Too often they look exactly like what they are: glossy plastic little people. What's the answer? Well, we weather everything else; why not our people too?

Perhaps the term "weather" isn't quite inclusive enough for the process we're about to describe. Yes, people do get dirty and worn, but by our process we are also able to create a sense of distance as well as emphasize shade and shadow and details that are lost by our low lighting levels. And best of all, we can achieve these effects without elaborate materials and without the rock-steady nerves generally needed for this kind of work.

The first thing we need is some scale figures. There are several brands on the market, and most of them are quite good. They may be painted or unpainted. Keep an eye out for proper proportions and lots of detail (wrinkles on clothes, pockets, etc.). If they are unpainted, paint them first. Don't get fancy — stock flesh for faces and hands, solid colors for the clothes, and so on. Don't worry about shade and shadow, eyes, buttons, and

Compare the unweathered figures with the weathered ones. The unweathered figures have a glossy one-dimensional look to them. Notice how the wrinkles are more pronounced in the weathered figures, giving the effect of shade and shadow. The faces also seem more detailed than they really are.

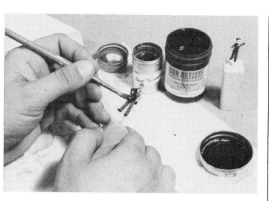

Fig. 1. Above. Both materials and technique are shown in this photo. Paint, paper towels, thinner, brush, and figure are all it takes. Simply brush the paint (antiquing stain) on the figure, covering it completely. **Fig. 2. Below.** After about 30 seconds or so (not critical) selectively wipe off areas to be highlighted, leaving the remainder to dry in cracks and crevasses. When happy with the look, spray the figure with a matt fixative.

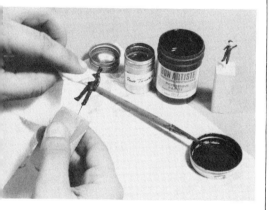

The sign for Rudnick's Manufacturing came from our author's telephone book and is affixed with carpet tape.

Signs from the Yellow Pages

BY LOU SASSI

I WAS TRYING to think of an easy way to make signs for model buildings when I literally stumbled across the answer — a telephone book left lying on the kitchen floor by one of my sons! As I regained consciousness I found myself staring at some advertisements in the Yellow Pages. Delighted by my discovering a ready source of signs, I wondered how I could attach them to structures on my HO layout. A little experimentation showed the advantages of using two-way carpet tape and the kind of cardboard found on the back of sketch pads.

Here's the technique in a nutshell: First, find an ad that fits your business in size and type. Cut it out and set it aside. Next, cut two pieces of carpet tape and a piece of cardboard slightly larger than your proposed sign. Stick one piece of carpet tape to the front of the cardboard, the other to the rear. Peel the protective backing from the piece of tape on the front and apply the sign. Now, with scissors or a razor blade, cut the entire assembly to your desired size. Remove the backing from the tape on the rear of the cardboard and stick the whole mess to the unsuspecting building. Weather the face of the sign with pastels and then stand back to admire your handiwork. ⚙

other details for now; just concentrate on the basics.

The only materials you'll need are shown in fig. 1: "antiquing" stains, paint thinner, a brush, paper towels, and figures. Bon Artiste stains are available in most craft stores and come in a variety of shades. We used Mediterranean Black and Honey Maple.

Brush the stain onto your figures with a medium brush (nos. 3 or 5) in a sloppy manner. No need to be neat. Completely cover the figure. Wait about 30 seconds (no hurry), and begin wiping it off with a paper towel scrap, as shown in fig. 2. The stain will remain in the cracks, wrinkles, button holes, under the chin, around the eyes, and so forth. This brings out the detail and creates highlights, shade, and shadow where you want it. Compare the weathered and unweathered people in the photos at left.

Nothing about this process is critical. If you feel you have wiped off too much, do it again. It's just that simple! You will notice that the stain darkens the figure somewhat overall, so you may want to use slightly lighter colors in the beginning painting.

The last step is to spray the figure with a matt fixative and place it on your layout. In no time at all you will have a variety of well painted figures that look as weather-worn and natural as any building or boxcar on your layout. ⚙

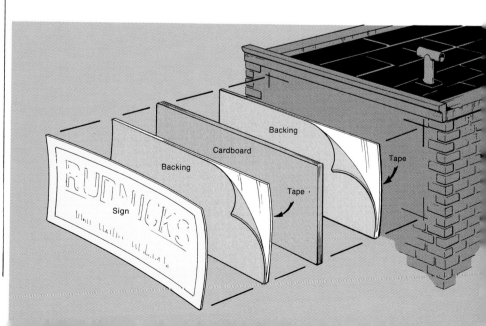

The loading dock of the local beverage distributor yields a wealth of colorful clutter. Actually the scene was staged with photo cutouts on a G scale diorama. All the original signs were found at a flea market.

Authentic advertising from photographs

Use your camera to make signs for any scale

BY CHRIS COMPORT
PHOTOS BY THE AUTHOR

SIGNS CAN SET the era, mood, and location of a model scene. The printed word, whether a "shingle," a billboard, or a poster, sets a time in history and expresses the character of that time. For me, the character of my modeling is expressed by the multitude of period advertisements on my 1920s-era On3 module.

Several manufacturers like Chooch, Woodland Scenics, and Vintage Reproductions have begun to provide dry transfers and printed sheets of more common signs. However, I've found many signs that belong on my railroad out in the real world.

Instead of waiting and hoping that a manufacturer will provide me with miniature replicas of these signs, I've used photos of real signs to add these eye-catching advertisements to my O scale module. If you have a 35-mm single lens reflex (SLR) camera, you too can begin to dress up a model scene with signs.

FINDING THE SUBJECTS

It's not hard to find signs to photograph for our purposes. Those of you who prefer modern railroading have it the easiest because modern signs are everywhere. Others who, like me, model the steam era have to look a little harder.

I've found a great variety of vintage advertising at antiques stores and flea markets. I've even stumbled across retailers, like the store in fig. 1, specializing in reproductions of old signs hawking everything from food to farm implements.

CAMERA, FILM, LIGHTING

Before heading out on a sign safari, you'll need to gather some equipment. You'll need a good 35-mm SLR camera with a 50-mm lens. This lens or one with a longer focal length will render all the edges of the sign nearly parallel, even at full frame. Wide-angle lenses less than 40 mm distort straight lines and shouldn't be used. A variable focal length zoom lens, say 50 to 100 mm, will give you additional flexibility in sizing signs for your needs.

Choose a fairly fast color print film of around 200 ISO rating, as it will allow you to shoot in lower light levels but not be as grainy as 400 ISO film. As for brands, Kodacolor Gold will render fairly reasonable color in both sun and artificial light. The color shift from mismatched lighting and film will be imperceptible when the final product is cut from the paper. If that shift is objectionable, most 1-hour labs can make a corrected print with the color balanced in the printing process.

EXPOSURE

When shooting signs, the lighting conditions will vary from bright sun, to shadow, to fluorescent light, and even to "available darkness." A flash unit may be useful for the last case, but care must be taken to eliminate glare from a frontal shot. To minimize glare from the flash, use an extension cable and move the flash as far as possible to either

Fig. 2 GRID

Exact size final print in viewfinder

	Approximate scale dimensions	
	x	y
N	16'-6"	23'-0"
HO	9'-0"	12'-6"
S	7'-0"	9'-6"
O	5'-0"	7'-0"
G	2'-6"	3'-6"
	2x	2y
N	33'-0"	46'-0"
HO	18'-0"	25'-0"
S	14'-0"	19'-0"
O	10'-0"	14'-0"
G	5'-0"	7'-0"

Fig. 1. SOURCE MATERIAL. The Antique Market-place in Arlington, Tex., is a nostalgia-oriented mall.

Fig. 3. TOOLS. Simple tools are all that's needed beyond camera and film. Chris uses small, sharp scissors, a single-edge razor blade, a sanding block, and 0000 steel wool.

side of the camera. Angle it at 45 degrees to the surface of the sign.

Bracket your exposures. In other words, shoot additional frames an f-stop on either side of the normal meter reading. For manual cameras, first establish the proper setting for the shutter speed and aperture; after each exposure, move the f-stop ring a "click" to the left and right of normal. Most automatic 35-mm SLR cameras have an override dial that allows bracketing — check your camera's instruction booklet for more details.

Since depth of field isn't critical, you can use the lower-numbered f-stops (f/2, f/3.5) to allow faster shutter speeds. Precise focusing is still required. One final note on camera positioning: Try your best to keep the film in your camera in a plane parallel with the sign. This will make the sign edges parallel and avoid a keystone effect.

SIZING YOUR PICTURES

Figure 2 represents the standard $3\frac{1}{2}$" x 5" color print as well as the average

viewfinder divided into eight equal parts, each part being a single "X" and "Y" unit. The table roughly translates the X and Y dimensions into scale feet for your convenience in sizing signs before shooting. Although exact scale size isn't critical, it may help you compose wall-size ads or billboards.

For very small signs you can stand farther back and shoot groups, but always try to maintain parallel planes. Large outdoor signs, such as highway exits, billboards, and business signs, may be better shot with a telephoto from ground level to avoid distortion. Commit the X and Y dimensions for your scale to memory, or drop a note in your camera bag.

TRIM AND FINISH

With the signs captured on film, it's time to have the film processed. In this day of jumbo prints, you may have to do a little looking to find a lab that makes $3\frac{1}{2}$" x 5" glossy prints. Matte-finish prints have texture that's unacceptable for our needs.

Figure 3 shows the tools you'll need to turn photos into signs. Use fine 0000 steel wool to remove the gloss from the glossy prints before trimming to size. Trim the signs using a pair of small, sharp scissors.

The thickness of the photo paper will make signs seem out of scale in HO or N scales. A simple solution is slicing into a corner of the sign between the layers with a single-edge razor blade. The emulsion layer will easily peel from the other paper layers. To thin a sign even further, sand the back with fine sandpaper on a block or tabletop.

The signs can now be attached to buildings, put on posts, or just set out behind the sign maker's shop. You can spray the signs with a light dusting of Testor's Dullcote and weather them if you want.

With nostalgia sweeping the nation, you'll occasionally find a dealer selling nothing but reproduction signs of yesteryear. You'll be surprised to find that one roll of film will yield more signs than model zoning codes allow. ✺

Signs of the times

Ads from old magazines can date your layout

BY CHARLES NICKLE

FOR MANY model railroaders, one of the more enjoyable challenges of the hobby is that of re-creating the illusion of a specific time period on their layout. They operate only period rolling stock and engines, they include buildings from their period or older, they use liberal quantities of period cars and trucks, and they put signs and other lettering around the layout to reflect the period. But finding or creating appropriate signs is often the toughest job of all.

Of course, you can go to your local hobby shop and find packets of signs in all the popular scales; unfortunately, these packages don't always have *exactly* what you want for *your* layout. This was the problem I had with my 1930s layout. But then one day, while I was browsing through the bargain section of a local used-book store, I found a source for scale signs and billboards that are authentic-looking and that represent my period — stacks of old magazines. I suspect that rummage and garage sales would also be good sources for old periodicals.

Most of the magazines I bought cost about $2 to $3 each. Each one can supply as many as a dozen or so assorted billboards, fence signs, posters, and placards. A bonus that you shouldn't overlook is the stories and photos. They can provide you with interesting and helpful information for modeling your period.

The publications that are the most fertile for my period are *National Geographic, Post,* and *Fortune* because they were widely circulated in the mid-1930s.

Once you have the magazines home, go to the layout and select the locations and sizes you want for your signs. Then, in a piece of blank paper, cut a hole the size of the space to be filled. Using this as a guide, thumb through the magazine checking for likely ads to convert. When you spot one — and *before* you start cutting — be sure to check what's on the page behind it. All too often a better ad, or part of one, is on the back of one you just cut out.

If the ad is printed in color, all you have to do is cut it out and fit it into its new home. Most of the ads from my period are in black and white. Some of them I use as is (see the Kellogg's billboard in the photo); others I tint with a felt-tip pen (like the Pennzoil ad). If you decide to color a black-and-white ad this way, be careful; the colors tend to bleed.

When the ad is ready for mounting on the layout, any of several bonding materials can be used. I use rubber cement, but any of the spray bonding materials would work just as well.

Once in place, the sign can be weathered. Pastel chalks work well because they can be wiped off without damaging the ad if the first try doesn't turn out. I generally don't seal the pastels since I have no need to touch the signs, but a coat of flat-finish sealer would do the trick if you feel it's necessary.

So, if you model a specific period, don't keep the fact hidden; advertise it with billboards and posters from old magazines. ✿

Dry-transfer signs

Easy, professional-looking signs for any industry

Neatly done chimney and main building signs provide identification and a nice finishing touch to this kitbashed industry on the author's HO scale layout. Such signs also help visiting operators.

BY LOU SASSI

GOOD-LOOKING SIGNS are an important means of adding realism to miniature structures. This sign-making technique is one I learned over the phone from my friend Dick Elwell. He got it from George Sellios during a visit to George's well-known HO scale Franklin & South Manchester. Despite its convoluted history, this sign-making method is so impressive that I just had to pass it on.

PAINTING

The Proctor Scale Co. is a reasonably large complex of kitbashed HO scale Magnuson buildings, with a Heljan Ford Motor Co. kit tacked on for good measure. I needed two signs, one horizontal and one vertical, to identify the business. The same technique was used for both signs, so I'm just going to discuss the vertical one here. These techniques also work well for other scales.

I began with a Cibilo Crossing cast-plaster octagonal chimney. Although these come painted, I sprayed mine with the same Sherwin-Williams Terra Cotta enamel I used for the brick color on the other structures. After waiting for about 15 minutes, I brush-painted 50 scale feet of one face of the stack with Floquil Engine Black.

LETTERING

As soon as the paint had dried (turned flat), I applied Woodland Scenics DT-506 white railroad Roman dry-transfer lettering. In this instance, I used the 3/8" letters (the largest on the sheet) for my HO smokestack.

Applying dry transfers can be a tricky business. I started at the top of the stack and worked down, using the applied letter as a guide to space the next one. To do this, I find the letter I need on the transfer sheet and then align the next higher row of letters (still on the sheet) with the one on the stack. See fig. 1.

As I'm positioning the letter, I slip the backing sheet between the model and the carrier sheet, leaving only the desired letter in contact. This protects against an undesired transfer of letters by finger pressure while I'm holding everything in place. When the letter is positioned properly, I rub the transfer sheet with a dull no. 2 pencil to apply the letter.

This spacing technique also works for horizontal lettering. Just position the letter to be applied so it's left or right of the previously applied letter. I use the spacing between the printed letters (on the transfer sheet) to guide the spacing between items and align the bottom edges. If a letter goes on wrong, I use a piece of masking tape to lift it off so I can try again.

After I'd finished applying the lettering, I brushed on a generous coat of India ink thinned with alcohol. I use a mix of 1 teaspoon of ink to 1 pint of rubbing alcohol. Once the ink stain had dried, I brushed on a mortar mix of 20 percent gray latex paint to 80 percent water, as shown in fig. 2, and let it dry.

That's it. The entire sign-making procedure takes about an hour, but the results certainly make the effort worthwhile. If you want more variety, check art supply and craft shops for other styles, colors, and sizes of dry transfers. You'll be amazed at what's available. ◊

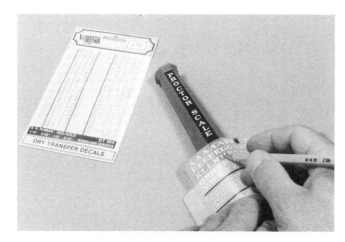

Fig. 1. LETTERING, Above. The author uses the transparent carrier sheet to help align the transfer letters. **Fig. 2. WASHES, Right.** After the ink stain, thinned latex paint is applied to simulate mortar.

In these two photographs, which were taken by the author, we see one of the scale billboards that he has constructed using the plans and the techniques described in this article.

Highway billboards from the 1930s and '40s

Add a bit of the past to your layout

BY STANLEY REYNOLDS

SINCE THE 1920s, advertising billboards have been one of the more noticeable items of scenery along streets and highways. That fact, along with the color and interest billboards add, makes them worthwhile elements for any layout.

To make modeling billboards easier, MODEL RAILROADER has published reproductions in various scales (for examples, see the November 1977, January 1979, and February 1980 issues). But those came from the postwar decades. Here you'll find some earlier ones and an explanation of how billboards were constructed in the 1930s and '40s.

In the mid-1940s I helped build and post billboards. At that time their appearance and construction had hardly changed in 20 years. However, in 1950 the Outdoor Advertising Association, which sets the standards for billboards, modified their specifications. Since then, billboards have remained about the same.

The methods I describe pertain to billboards put up between 1920 and 1950. Of course, there are probably a few of the older ones still standing in out-of-the-way places, so this design could be used to a limited extent on a layout set in more recent times.

BOARDS AND THEIR LOCATION

Let's first clarify the differences between posted paper billboards and painted signboards. They often appear similar and may be owned by the same firm. However, the paper posters are a standard size and are mounted on standardized boards, while painted signboards may be any size. The branch of outdoor advertising that deals with painted posted paper signs is a franchise type of operation, and only one firm will operate in a particular area.

Most billboards are put up in vacant lots or odd corners that can't be used for other purposes. Poster companies choose these locations to avoid paying high rent. To save money they try to put up more than one board in a place, though that depends on the space available and the level of passing traffic. This last factor, the potential viewers of the signs, has the most influence when companies select their sites.

Main streets and highways have always been the typical locations for billboards. Rail lines with commuter service and interurban and streetcar lines have also been used. The number and arrangement of the boards generally depends on the size and shape of the available location. Since the criteria for sign locations haven't changed, when choosing sites on your layout look at where you see real billboards placed.

CONSTRUCTION

The drawings should give you a good idea of how billboards were constructed. Usually it was not possible to buy lumber that was long enough, so the material was spliced. Posts were generally spliced (at the top end) with two 2" x 6" pieces scabbed on, while stringers were spliced and had another piece of the same material scabbed on the back (fig. 1).

Where I worked, back bracing was often attached to cedar posts set in the ground. Sometimes, especially if the board locations were low or damp, the main posts were spliced to heavier cedar posts at the bottom. Elsewhere, creosoted posts or lumber were used (see fig. 2).

The 2" x 4" footrail at the back top provided workers with a place to stand while putting up sheet-metal posting surface sections and the molding and cap pieces. The corner irons shown in fig. 3

were light-gauge sheet metal with a floral leaf design stamped on. They eliminated mitering the corners of the molding.

The posting surface was made of light-gauge galvanized sheet metal fastened to a 1" x 4" frame as shown in fig. 4, with the frame held together by sheet-metal splices. There were five panels to each board.

Although grating at the bottom of a billboard was more common than horizontal strips, it would be harder to model. When grating was used at the bottom of side-by-side installations, it would also be used between billboards. When horizontal strips were used there, vertical strips would be found between boards.

PAINT AND SIGNS

Billboards were painted a standard color called "poster green," a bright shade much like kelly green. Everything except the metal posting surface would be painted on boards positioned so that viewers could see all of them. When the rear didn't show, only the front might be painted, with the back and bracing left to weather. New paint was shiny, but soon weathered to a chalky appearance.

The company's name was added, usually in white lettering on a black background with a white border. A fairly ornate style of lettering was common. The signs on present-day posterboards are similar to those on older ones.

BUILDING A MODEL

The drawings show the boards as they were built, though they can be modified as necessary. Modelers can build to any scale from 12" = 12" on down and can include as much detail as desired. A model in the foreground might be built in complete detail, while one in the background could be simplified.

In the larger scales, an absolute scale model would be possible using available lumber. A more practical approach would be to use a piece of light cardboard the size of the billboard. An appropriate poster from a magazine could be glued to the front. Then the molding frame could be built around it. Back detail could be added and stringers and posts attached.

Making the grating at the bottom would be a challenge, especially in the smaller scales. Building it piece by piece from small stripwood would be time-consuming. Instead, you might try punched wood grating, which was once available for constructing model ships. Or you could build horizontal strips, which is just as prototypical if not as common.

My own model is built to TT scale (.1" = 1' or 1:120). It represents a new billboard ready to be posted, which is why the metal posting surface shows. I made that out of aluminum foil (dull side out) affixed to each side with rubber cement. Next, I built section framing from scale 1 x 4 strips and attached stringers and posts. I used a small piece of balsa for the base and glued Woodland Scenics grass to the surface.

The back posts were sanded to a taper and left rough to simulate real cedar ones. Then I stained them with iodine. I erected the sign and posts on the base and attached the back bracing. I built the back braces and subbracing for each as a unit of uniformity.

After attaching the strips of grating, I painted the front of the billboard with Pactra Leaf Green enamel. This leaves a fairly glossy surface, but my model is of a new board. Use green railroad paints to get the flat appearance of a weathered one. Then I made a company name using a Leroy lettering set with white ink on a black background. I attached the sign to the grating, which completed the model.

To install a billboard on a layout, you can put it on a base or runner and build it into the scenery. Or you can drill small holes into the scenery and install it in prototypical fashion.

ADVERTISERS

Now you're ready for the fun, posting ads for your scale people (and real visitors) to look at. When I was posting boards the chief advertiser was Coca-Cola. Other soft drink bottlers advertised, but not as much as Coke. Oil companies were also large advertisers, led by Gulf, Humble (now Exxon), and Conoco. These mostly advertised their brands of gasoline. Auto makers advertised widely before World War II. During and after the war, when the demand for cars was so great, they didn't need to.

Beers, both nationally distributed brands like Schlitz and various local ones, were commonly advertised. Among consumer items, there were billboards for Bulova watches, especially around Christmas, and Levi Strauss work clothes (this was before jeans became high style!).

Tobacco companies were also important advertisers, with the leading brands being Camels, Lucky Strike, and Old Gold. Other popular ones, such as Phillip Morris, Pall Mall, and Kool, were also featured on many billboards.

Then as now, an advertising campaign often coincided with the introduction of a new product. The same ads might be found on billboards and in magazines, which is why old copies of *Life, Saturday Evening Post,* and *Look* are good sources of posters for model billboards. Use your imagination and a little common sense — Don't go advertising computers on a layout set in the 1930s or Packards and Hudsons on one set in the '80s!

FINAL SUGGESTIONS

The company I worked for used a portable scaffold, hung from the billboard, to post from. Other firms had their workers stand on the ground and use long-handled brushes. To make your layout more interesting you might try adding a crew and a partially complete board.

Billboards are a very visible item of scenery, especially in urban areas and along main travel routes. Adding a few in selected spots on your model railroad will add to its realism and enable you to capture the feel of another era. ⚲

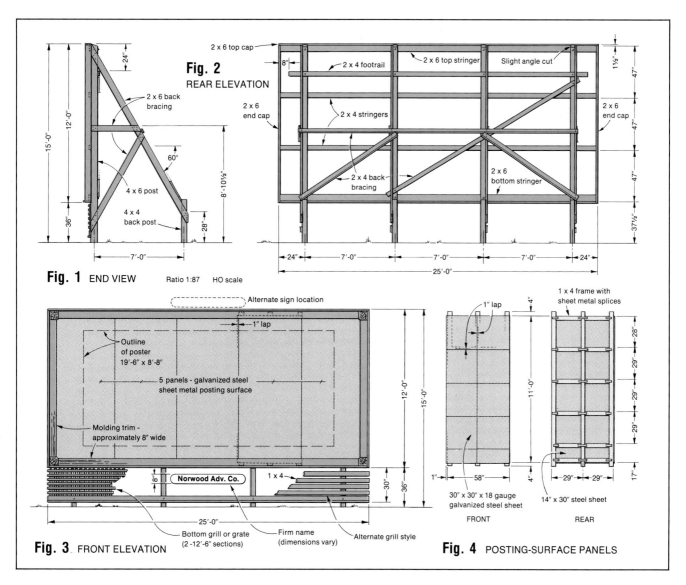

Fig. 1 END VIEW   Ratio 1:87   HO scale

Fig. 2 REAR ELEVATION

Fig. 3 FRONT ELEVATION

Fig. 4 POSTING-SURFACE PANELS

Look carefully down the street under the viaduct. Are you able to spot the mirrors? No backwards signs or head-on collisions in this town! Photo by the author.

Mirror magic

Double mirrors straighten things out

BY CHARLES LAMAN

WE LOOK into mirrors every day and are conditioned to accept a reversed image where left is right, right is left, and words read backwards. But that's not the way mirrors work on *my* layout. In that magical miniature world, left is left and right is right!

To explain what I've done we must go back to 1986, when I first saw George Sellios' layout, the HO scale Franklin & South Manchester, as part of a tour at the National Model Railroad Association's national convention. His beautiful poured concrete streets and sidewalks made me want to try modeling those features. [Articles on the F&SM have appeared in the April 1986, April 1987, January 1989, and March 1990 MODEL RAILROADER. — *Ed.*]

I decided to try out the poured concrete look on an Ntrak module that I

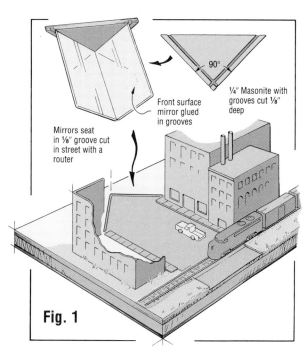

Fig. 1

90°

¼" Masonite with grooves cut ⅛" deep

Front surface mirror glued in grooves

Mirrors seat in ⅛" groove cut in street with a router

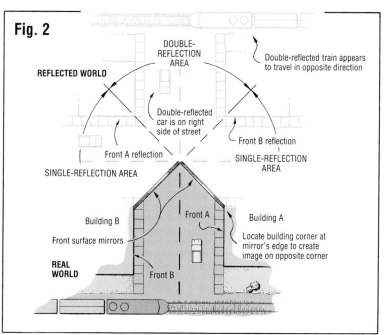

Fig. 2

REFLECTED WORLD

DOUBLE-REFLECTION AREA

Double-reflected train appears to travel in opposite direction

Double-reflected car is on right side of street

Front A reflection

Front B reflection

SINGLE-REFLECTION AREA

SINGLE-REFLECTION AREA

Building B

Front surface mirrors

Front A

Building A

Locate building corner at mirror's edge to create image on opposite corner

REAL WORLD

Front B

had acquired from Larry Hough (a fellow Northeast Ntrak member). To get started I had to tear up some blacktop roads; however, on the chance that I might not like the results, I decided to replace only the section between the track and the front of the module.

I removed the existing street right down to the plywood base and glued in a plaster casting of poured concrete street and sidewalk. I added a crossing shanty on one side of the road and a kitbashed station on the other. Trees, lights, grass, and other details completed the scene. The effect was just what I wanted. The poured concrete street and sidewalk conveyed the message that this was an old community that dated back at least to the 1930s.

WHERE DOES THE ROAD GO?

I displayed the module (modified only to this extent) at several shows and got a feeling that there was general approval of what I was doing. I laid in another length of cast-plaster street on the other side of the track with the same pleasing results. This was as far as I could go without making a decision: Was the road going to continue straight and run unrealistically into the skyboard in the back, or would it take a turn, like the road on the original module, and gracefully disappear?

As things turned out, I hadn't made enough of the street castings to effectively make a turn in the road. That left me worried that the end result would be something I really didn't like. There had to be something that could be done, but I didn't know what. The Philadelphia Eastern Ntrak Convention was getting closer, and I wanted to attend with this module as part of my four-module group. I spent many hours trying to figure out what to do. One thought kept coming back — What about mirrors?

I went to a glass supply house and bought an assortment of scrap mirror pieces, 2″ x 3″ to 3″ x 5″, to play around with. Typically, model railroaders have used mirrors to give the illusion that the track and/or scenery goes on twice as far as it really does. However, it didn't work here since reflected vehicles would be heading down the wrong side of the street, giving the illusion of multiple head-on collisions about to happen.

FINDING A SOLUTION

Eventually, the rest of the family got curious and started playing around with the mirrors. A few days later I heard, "Hey, Dad, come look at this." My sons had positioned two mirrors such that they made a 90-degree angle in the middle of the street. The reflected vehicles appeared on the correct side of the street! The more I looked, the more fascinated I became and realized that this could be the solution to my problem.

However, with ordinary mirrors, the reflecting surface is about ⅛″ behind the glass surface, creating a telltale line at the intersection of the two mirrors and at the street. I would have to have mirrors that reflected from the front surface rather than the rear. The Edmund Scientific Industrial Catalog had what I was looking for: first-surface mirrors (item no. P32,271).

I rushed off an order for two 3″ x 5″ mirrors. Upon their arrival I opened the box and placed the two mirrors at a 90-degree angle to each other. The intersection between the two could not be seen. Using an ordinary glass cutter, I cut the mirrors to the size I wanted.

Then, using a table saw, I cut ⅛″-deep grooves in a piece of ¼″-thick Masonite at exactly 90 degrees to each other (see fig. 1). I inserted the mirrors in the grooves and glued them together with silicone adhesive. Next, I cut grooves in the street with a router, using a car-

penter's framing square as a guide, and glued the other end of the mirrors in place with Elmer's carpenter's glue.

Unfortunately, that glue shrinks while drying, moving the mirrors out of alignment and causing distortion. I had to reposition the mirrors slightly, which I did by installing adjusting screws against wood wedges so that exactly 90 degrees could be maintained. Next time I'll use only silicone adhesive.

Buildings were positioned at the mirror's edges, forming corners with the reflected images. To hide the tops of the mirrors, I installed a deck girder bridge for elevated trolley service behind the buildings and over the street.

The overall effect was pleasing. With the mirrors I doubled the length of the street. Better yet, reflected vehicles ran on the right side of the street, reflected signs could be read directly, and reflected trains ran opposite to the direction of those on the module.

NOT WITHOUT A FLAW

A street intersection was also formed by the mirrors, but here the magic ended. The cross street is the result of only single reflection. Here, alas, the rules of an ordinary mirror apply. Signs are backwards, and vehicles are on the wrong side of the road. Careful placement of objects can minimize the problems. Vehicles can be positioned far enough away from the intersection so they aren't seen on the cross street; the same is true of signs. See fig. 2 to help you envision how this happens.

The irony of all this is that mirror usage was not part of the original plan, but a solution to a rather perplexing problem. Just imagine what could be done if a scene were initially planned using this mirror technique, or maybe using one-way mirrors for still other magical effects. ⊘

Scale tails

An easy way
to model cattails
in any scale

BY WILLIAM VINIKOUR
PHOTOS BY THE AUTHOR

CATTAILS can give your layout that extra bit of diversity that will help your ponds, streams, and sloughs stand out in the "field." In this article I'll explain an easy, inexpensive method to make realistic-looking cattail plants. For an investment of only about $10 you can make hundreds.

Cattails are one of the most widely distributed wetland plants. They commonly grow in drainage ditches along railroad tracks and on the shores of ponds and slow streams. In fact, they can even be found in areas where there are acidic coal mine drainages. Such habitats are found on many layouts, but cattails are rarely incorporated into these scenes. Modeling attempts at cattails usually involve the use of stiff, green brush bristles. While somewhat suitable for smaller scales, brush bristles give a less than desirable appearance to foreground scenes.

TECHNIQUES AND MATERIALS

To model more appealing cattails I have modified and expanded on a technique that's described in the book *Period Floral Designs in Miniature*. The photo below shows the supplies: various gauges of green craft (floral) wire, brown floral tape, Rock Quarry's fine logging ground debris (finely blended pecan shells), and preserved bulrush.

Preserved bulrush is available at craft stores that sell dried or preserved plants. In larger packages it goes by such names as strip grass, onion grass, and isolepsis. The bulrush is available in shades of green, brown, and reddish-brown. The browns are great for modeling fall through spring scenes, dead stands, ground litter from the previous year's growth, and muskrat lodges. You can also mix them in with the green material to indicate a few dead leaves.

CREATING THE ILLUSION

Before I get into "growing" cattails, a few notes are called for on prototype dimensions and artistic license in modeling. Cattail stands on the layout need only be in the approximate size range for the scale you are modeling. You don't have to obtain the precise prototypical width and height of each leaf. Instead, aim for the correct illusion.

Cattails tend to stand 4 to 6 feet high, though one hybrid grows as tall as 12 feet. The leaves are generally less than an inch wide, but for modeling appearances they can be several scale inches wide. The flowering part of the spike consists of the pistil (female) below and the stamen (male) above. Both portions range in length from 6" to 12". In scales smaller than O, you need model only the pistil. Modelers in the larger scales may wish to have some cattails with both flowering portions.

ASSEMBLY PROCEDURE

Assembling the cattails is quite simple — a great job to do while watching TV. First cut the wire about an actual ¼" longer than the scale 6- to 8-foot lengths required. The extra length will be inserted into the modeling base. For larger scales that require a thicker gauge wire, you'll need to file the ends, grind them smooth, and touch them up with green paint. If you want dead cattails, first paint the wire a tannish brown and let it dry.

Next, cut off some strips of floral tape. Floral tape comes in rolls that are ½" wide. This is just right for G scale, as it will give a scale 12"-tall flowering spike. For smaller scales, cut the tape into narrower strips. I generally cut it into ⅛" strips for HO scale. Again, we want to create an illusion, so it's not vital to adhere to prototype dimensions.

Now hold the tape at each end and stretch it out. This seems to bring out the stickiness of the tape. Fold an end of the tape around the wire, and pinch the tape together. Then wrap it around the wire two or three times. Cut the tape near the wire, and press down the free end of the tape. If not prepositioned, slide the tape near the top of the wire, being sure to leave a few scale inches of wire exposed above the tape.

Brush dilute white glue over the tape, and dip it into the logging debris. Besides hiding the tape, the debris give nice texture to the cattail and suggest that the flowering portion is going to seed.

INSTALLATION

Now you're ready to put your cattails on your layout. Start by drilling a number of holes into the area where you want your cattail stand. This is similar to adding trees and bushes and should be done after your terrain has been completed. For HO scale, the hole should be about ¹⁄₁₆" in diameter.

Cut off a group of about six to eight pieces of bulrush to insert in each hole. For the smaller scales use the thinner leaves (wider leaves may be cut thinner). I vary my leaf length from about a scale foot taller than the spike to several scale feet shorter. Dab the end of the bulrush bunch into white glue, and insert into the hole. A cattail spike is then inserted in a similar manner.

Repeat this planting procedure until your wetland is seeded with cattails. Remember, cattails can be found in many low-lying areas, even those that are not saturated with water the year round.

Maintaining your cattail stand would be similar to what's done for lichen or any preserved plant. You'll have to apply some glycerin every few years. I suggest misting the plants with a 1:4 mixture of glycerine to denatured alcohol.

I have shown my cattails to model railroaders as well as fellow biologists. Both groups were impressed with the realism achieved by this method. ✿

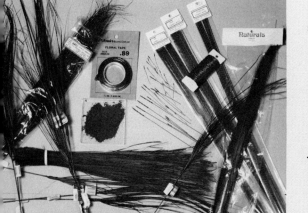

Bill of materials

Supplies
  Brown floral tape
  Green floral wire
    20 gauge for G scale
    22 gauge for O scale
    24 gauge for S smaller
  Preserved bulrush
    brown for dead plants
    green for live ones
  Rock Quarry's logging ground debris

Tools
  Hand drill
  Scissors
  White glue
  Wire cutters

This photo, taken by Chris on his layout, shows that his method of modeling pines produces authentic-looking trees.

Pine trees for your layout

A new way to make realistic pine foliage

BY CHRIS MC CHESNEY

ANYONE modeling logging operations has been faced with the problem of finding realistic foliage for coniferous trees. My brother and I tried working with asparagus fern, but found it tedious and the results far from convincing. Nor did we like caspia branches, as their shape and texture made our trees look more like deciduous ones than coniferous. Just when we were ready to give up and start modeling Arizona deserts, a new product came on the market that's helping us turn our dream of a layout covered with thick pines into reality.

I'm talking about Finescale Forest, which contains ferns that have been preserved and dyed to natural green tones. It's made by Joel Bradgon, P. O. Box 487, Georgetown, CA 95634. The beauty of this product is that the fronds have the same shape and texture of the real thing, right down to the individual pine-cones and needles. It's also thick, which means it fills a balsa trunk faster and more easily than caspia or asparagus fern. The process of making trees is similar to others, though I've come up with a few shortcuts to make it even simpler to add good-looking and realistic conifer-ous trees to layouts in any scale.

TRUNK

To make an average size tree for my layout, I start with a strip of ¼″ balsa that's about 6″ long. Instead of an X-acto knife, I use a new single-edge razor blade to make the cuts in the trunk. With this blade I can control where the cuts go by bringing the blade closer to or farther from the edge of the wood.

With the base of the trunk pointed down, I trim the corners to make a round trunk. Then I begin to carve the entire trunk. I hold the base with my left hand and draw the blade down the trunk with my right. Keep a constant taper as you go down the trunk by using 1″ strokes with the blade, always check-ing to see that the taper is correct. If the blade begins to wander into the middle of the trunk, slowly draw it out at an angle.

After you've carved the trunk, don't sand it; sanding only makes model trees look like tapered rods with branches sticking out! Adding the bark texture will take away any cutting lines. To make the bark, I put a hacksaw blade into a vise (with the blade pointing up) and carefully draw the trunk from base to tip across the blade. The effect is much like using a razor saw to give wood a grainy look.

Next, drill a no. 65 hole into the cen-ter of the bottom of the trunk. Insert some wire of the appropriate diameter into the trunk, and trim it to about ¼″. The final step is to stain the trunk with Floquil Natural Pine (no. 110722).

GREEN STUFF

Now we'll add vegetation to the bare trunk. First spread some of the Fine-scale Forest material onto a sheet of pa-per so each piece can be seen. Have two pin vises ready, one with a no. 65 drill for the large-foliage branches and an-other with a no. 70 drill for the smallest foliage branches. Also have a dab of white glue ready to use.

With the trunk secured into a piece of Styrofoam, drill two holes one-third to one-half way up the trunk. The holes should be opposite each other yet slightly apart both vertically and horizontally. Trim the back of the foliage branch to the desired length, dab the end into the white glue, and stick it into the trunk.

Continue with the next two pieces by placing them above and perpendicular to the first two pieces. Do this until you've reached the tip. There may not be enough room to add two more branches; if not, drill one hole at the extreme end of the trunk so that the top of the wood is not visible. When everything has dried the tree is ready to be painted. I should point out that one bag of the Finescale Forest material is enough to make about 30 pines that are 6″ high.

SPECIAL EFFECTS

Making some unusual trees will accent the other trees in your forest. To get ideas study the shapes of trees in a forest. You'll notice that on hills some trees have curved trunks. On water edges and cliffs, trees can be found with trunks that have a complete curve. Also, trees can be found with their trunks rotted out.

Whatever tree you decide to build, it will take some planning. Either visually or mentally, make notes of where the cuts in the trunk should be made. For curved or bent trees use a bigger balsa strip to accommodate the curve. For rotted trees rip out the area you don't want with a razor blade. Recently I found that inserting the finest part of actual tree roots to the base of the foliage helps represent the lower dead branches of pine trees.

When modelers look at most hand-made trees, they wonder how long it would take to make all the trees needed on their layout. That's not the approach I take. After building more than 130 trees I have streamlined my techniques so that a new pine normally takes only 12 minutes to make. One shortcut in-volves drilling each hole at a slight an-gle. That way, the branches overlap more and fill more space quickly.

I also build my trees in an assembly-line fashion, making trunks in batches of a dozen so they're ready whenever I feel like building some trees. When I do build I make three to seven trees and later plant them in groups, which fills a forest rapidly. I am very pleased with my results with the Finescale Forest mate-rial, and the effort put into each tree is justified by the beautiful rewards. ✿

These trees were made using the methods outlined here. The author used mirrors to create the dense and dark effect.

Creating realistic conifers

How to make realistic evergreens without spending a bundle

BY LASZLO DORA

PHOTOS BY THE AUTHOR

IN MY VIEW, a model layout is not complete unless it has adequate scenery, which in most cases includes trees. Unfortunately, trees just don't seem too popular, for many layouts lack adequate numbers of this essential scenic detail. This is understandable, because making a high-quality tree can be both costly and time-consuming.

I'd like to share a method of making coniferous trees that are extremely realistic, yet end up costing less than quality kit trees. With this method a great number of tree varieties can be modeled. The following instructions may seem long and complicated, but don't worry — it's all quite simple.

Trees, like locomotives and rolling stock, differ from each other. That's why, unless you have the tree you intend to model in front of you, I recommend borrowing or purchasing a book or two. I've come across many interesting books about trees, with the softcover set of two field guides put out by the Audubon Society being especially worthwhile.

The Audubon Society Field Guide to North American Trees contains volumes on the eastern and the western regions; together, they cover more than 680 trees and include hundreds of detailed color photographs, drawings, and maps, along with a complete description of each type of tree. The description includes height, trunk diameter, location, color, habitat, and popular uses of the tree. In short, everything a modeler needs to know. The pair of books is available in many bookstores and costs about $30.

SELECTING AND PRESERVING FERNS

Almost all the materials necessary for making trees are easy to obtain. The main ones are balsa and assorted ferns. I should note that I did encounter problems finding some of the ferns. Luckily, there are so many types of ferns that some can be substituted for those that are hard to locate.

Figure 1 shows what some of these ferns look like. In these two pictures only a part of a typical branch is shown. Two of the ferns on the left side in fig. 1 are from the asparagus that we eat, and from here on I will refer to this as "edible asparagus fern." In southern Ontario I pick it in the wild, but your florist, grocer, or seed dealer should be able to help you get some. This fern is most suitable for making trees with long drooping branches. Air fern, which is not shown, is similar to edible asparagus fern.

Nearly all florists carry fine asparagus fern, which is usually arranged with roses. This fern is best suited for the construction of young coniferous trees. Some larger trees may be modeled from this fern, but doing so is time-consuming since the fern is extremely fine.

Tiki fern is another common fern used by florists. This fern is not as dense as the asparagus fern and is suited for only a few types of trees.

Ming fern has been the most difficult to locate. I've had to go to several florists to find some, but the effort has always been worth it because this fern is good for making so many types of trees. It's especially suited for trees that are dense and hard to see through.

Before going much farther I should mention that some florists stock certain ferns only on a seasonal basis. Ferns should be fresh when you purchase them and will remain so for over two weeks if kept in fresh water.

After that time, however, the ferns will start to dry out and become extremely fragile. Preserve them by soaking in a solution consisting of 1 part

Fig. 1. Left: Here are four different types of ferns that the author uses to simulate tree foliage. From left to right: two examples of edible asparagus fern, asparagus fern used in floral arrangements, tiki fern, and ming fern. **Fig. 2. Above:** Here's a batch of asparagus fern, enough to make about 40 trees, ready to be preserved by heating it in a mix of water and glycerine.

Fig. 3. Tree trunk coloration is important. Silver paint was used for the bark of this silver fir.

glycerine (available at pharmacies) to 2 parts water. The glycerine will drive the water out of the fern, and the fern will not dry out. If you're preserving tiki, air, or asparagus ferns, carefully pack large amounts into a shallow pan as shown in fig. 2. When preserving ming fern, pack it as densely as possible, but avoid flattening its round spherical clusters. When the ferns are in the pan, pour in the solution, making sure that the ferns are submerged. Heat the solution until vapors rise and it's extremely hot yet not boiling. (Boiling will soften and ruin most ferns.) Keep it in this state for a few minutes and then remove from the heat and let it cool. Once the solution's cool, remove the ferns from the pan and place them over old newspapers to absorb any runoff.

The glycerine/water solution may be used again if you replenish any glycerine that was lost. Usually this means adding a few tablespoons of glycerine to the solution.

TREE CONSTRUCTION

Once I have determined which tree to model, I use the following procedure to build it. First, carve a tapered tree trunk from a strip of balsa. Use a motor tool or sandpaper to finish it to the desired shape. If the tree has coarse bark exposed, run coarse sandpaper along the trunk, applying enough pressure to form

deep grooves. Then gently sand it with fine sandpaper to remove any scales.

Next, paint the tree trunk. I like using water-based paints, but feel free to use other types. The Audubon Society's books have closeup photos of each type of trunk, and I simply paint mine to match. This may require coats of various colors. If the trunk being modeled has shiny scales, rub on a wash of thinned silver. Figure 3 shows a tree trunk in detail.

The trick behind modeling individual types of trees is to build the proper shape by using the appropriate fern and placing it correctly.

I assemble the branches from the top down. Doing so ensures that there is finger room and reduces the danger of breaking the trunk. Should a trunk snap, be sure to follow the simple repair procedure shown in fig. 4. Remove the head of a sewing pin, sharpen it on a file, and place it into one of the broken ends. Then apply white glue to the ends of both pieces and join them. Use pliers and tweezers to make the job easier. Let the trunk dry for at least half an hour before continuing.

I often use a piece of ming fern for the crown, as space is limited at the top of the tapered trunk. Using a pin with a head, drill a hole by gently rotating it back and forth. Be careful because the wood is weakest at the tapered top and may

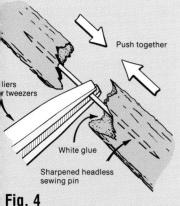

Fig. 4
REPAIRING BROKEN TRUNK

Push together

liers
tweezers

White glue

Sharpened headless
sewing pin

Bill of materials

Material	Use
Styrofoam	For holding tree trunks
Hard balsa	Tree trunks
Water-based paints	Painting tree trunks
Fine and coarse sandpaper	Finishing tree trunks
Glycerine	Preserving ferns
Ferns	Making tree branches
Edible asparagus	
Ming	
Tiki	
Fine asparagus	
Air	
Scissors, pins, tweezers	Branch assembly
White glue	To glue ferns into trunk
Spray glue	To glue turf material onto ferns
Fine and coarse ground foam	Adding "body" to foliage
Spray paints	Coloring trees

Fig. 5. The 4 steps in modeling a silver fir are shown in the photo above: (1) making the trunk, (2) adding edible asparagus fern, (3) adding ground foam, and (4) spray-painting the tree. To model the red cedar shown in the left photo, the author used ming fern. He made certain to give it extra applications of ground foam — first coarse and second fine.

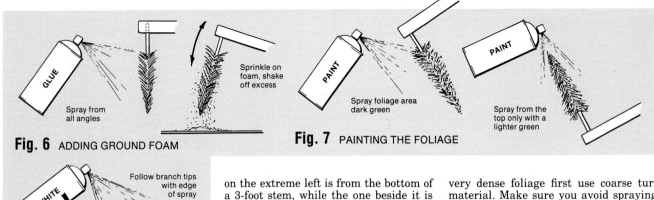

Fig. 6 ADDING GROUND FOAM

Spray from all angles

Sprinkle on foam, shake off excess

Fig. 7 PAINTING THE FOLIAGE

Spray foliage area dark green

Spray from the top only with a lighter green

Fig. 8

SNOW-COVERED TREES

WHITE

Follow branch tips with edge of spray

crack. Then dip the stem of the fern into white glue and place into the hole. If the wood is cracked, the glue will strengthen it. Use tweezers and hold the fern by the stem, close to the tip. Drill holes near where you're holding the wood.

Generally I precut the fern into various sizes, using the smaller and finer pieces at the top and the larger and stronger ones at the bottom where the branches are bigger and longer. In fig. 1 I purposely showed two bits of edible asparagus fern on the left side. The one

on the extreme left is from the bottom of a 3-foot stem, while the one beside it is the very top of a stem. Notice the difference? I try to use every bit of a fern. The tree should have a rough yet proper shape once the ferns are glued in place. Then trim it. Figure 5 shows two conifers at this stage.

The next step is to thicken the foliage by affixing ground foam to the fern branches. Firmly place the trunk into a foam base, as it will be sprayed with glue from all angles. Spray adhesives can be quite messy, and the fumes may be toxic. Check the label. Make sure there's adequate ventilation and use a respirator. Do the spraying in a paint booth or outside.

Most larger trees cannot be sprayed in one shot. Once one part of the tree is sprayed, sprinkle fine foam turf material onto that part. Tap the trunk so any unglued foam will fall off and continue on to the next section. Make sure that all the branches are covered on both top and bottom. The process is illustrated in fig. 6. If you can still see through the tree, give it another coat of turf material. For

very dense foliage first use coarse turf material. Make sure you avoid spraying the trunk.

PAINTING

By observing a tree you'll notice that the inside is darker due to shade within. To achieve the same effect with model trees, spray the entire tree with Colorado Green or another shade of dark green. Make sure that the inside is completely painted. Next, spray on a lighter green from the top as shown in fig. 7. I use automotive paints, which are quite inexpensive compared to hobby paints.

In the case of trees that have an additional tint, such as the blue spruce or silver fir, simply spray a "quick mist" of the required color on in the proper location. If you're not satisfied, paint it over.

When preserving ferns I usually set aside a bunch of the fine asparagus fern and let it dry out. Once dry the fern will drop its needles and only the branches will remain. I cut these up and use them to represent dead branches. They are glued in just like the other branches.

SNOW-COVERED TREES

Creating snow-covered trees requires two additional steps. First, select the completed tree that you wish to convert and set it back into the foam holder. Spray it with glue directly from the top of the tree and add a layer of fine turf material. Repeat this step two more times until you've created a thicker branch cover, though only where the snow would land.

Second, paint the tree as previously described. Spray white paint onto the tree directly from the top. The white paint should land onto the areas where the snow would land; that is, where the extra turf material was added. If the mist of white paint does not fully cover the lower areas, then keep the spray head as close as possible to the branches and make sure that only the edge of the spray mist touches the branch tips that need extra paint. Figure 8 should clarify this process. If you want the snow to sparkle, add a light mist of silver.

Experience has shown that a small tree can be made in less than ten minutes, while larger ones may take an hour or so, depending on how detailed they are. Ming fern tends to be the easiest to work with due to its "bushy" nature.

Three different types of evergreens that I've modeled are shown in fig. 9. I hope my article inspires you to try making some trees using this method. It's fun, and your efforts will create a layout with lots of good-looking trees. ◊

Fig. 9. Three examples of the many types of conifers modeled by the author. From left to right: a Colorado blue spruce (ming fern), a Norway spruce (asparagus fern), and a black spruce (ming fern).

A New York Central RS-3 rolls through a heavily forested (*i.e.*, "ragweeded") area on Lou Sassi's HO scale West Hoosic Division.

Using weeds for woods

Ragweed painted green does a nice imitation of trees

BY LOU SASSI
PHOTOS BY THE AUTHOR

ONCE THE BASIC SCENERY was completed on my HO scale Boston & Maine RR West Hoosic Division [featured in the July 1988 MODEL RAILROADER], I found it necessary to develop a technique for creating the heavily wooded countryside of the Northeast.

For the more detailed areas of the layout I relied on Les Jordan's method of making deciduous trees from cudweed. That method, described in the October 1979 issue of *Railroad Model Craftsman*, involves wrapping individual stems with masking tape, applying Liquid Steel (used in automotive repair) to form a trunk, and hand-painting the assembly. While this worked well for trees bearing close scrutiny, the thought of covering acres of HO real estate with these little devils gave me cold chills. It was clear some other way would have to be found.

Mother Nature came to the rescue. One afternoon in October, while driving past a field full of dry goldenrod, it struck me how closely this resembled the woods of the area in overall appearance.

Other HO scale modelers I know had taken a variety of weeds and covered them with ground foam to create forests. I liked the results but thought adding ground foam was an expensive and time-consuming step, especially since the texture of the weeds I'd found nicely resembled full-scale tree foliage. (Actually,

what you see as foliage on the weeds in October and November is the opened seed pods of the plant.) So why not just spray-paint the existing dried weeds and call it a day? That's exactly what I did.

A trip to the local K Mart yielded a half-dozen cans of dark green and avocado spray paint. Then, using a discarded piece of Styrofoam scenery, I jammed the weed stalks in place and had my son Adam spray them thoroughly with the green, then lightly with the avocado for highlighting.

After letting them dry for 24 hours, we trimmed each weed to remove some of the "drooping" that's common in goldenrod, and planted them in a hole pierced in the scenery base with a pocketknife. I use the "Easy Shell" scenery technique, explained in the April 1987 MR, which makes planting trees so easy. If you use plaster or Hydrocal as a base, you may need to drill holes for planting.

I don't glue my trees in place. The Easy Shell seems to hold everything firmly. If you prefer, add a small drop of white glue to each stalk before planting.

Now take all the material you've acquired from your trimming and spread it around the base of your trees and in your miniature fields to represent (you guessed it!) weeds. Secure these with a mixture of 3 parts water to 1 part white glue applied in an eyedropper. You see, besides being inexpensive, my technique has almost no waste.

You're now ready to stand back and enjoy the acres of HO scale forest you have just created at very little expense and in almost no time. ◊

The author's son Adam clips ragweed in the fall to use for an HO scale forest. Your allergist wouldn't recommend doing this during hay fever season!

Adam sprays the weeds (stuck in a Styrofoam base) with dark green and then avocado-colored paints. After clipping off some ends, he sticks them into the Easy Shell, and a forest is born.

Go fly a kite! (or an airplane)

Two easy projects for adding action to your layout

BY RICK SPANO

A S A CHILD I was fascinated watching the animated watchman snap in and out of the gatehouse as a train passed. Both Lionel and American Flyer had a version of this accessory. As much as this image remains fondly in my memory, though, it's not the type of animation I would like now on my layout — the action is too quick and unrealistic.

Oh, I would love to see a miniature gateman walk out and shine his lantern near the tracks as a model train approaches, but because of the technical difficulties I doubt that a realistic animated HO or N scale walking person will be produced in my lifetime. There are lots of other model situations that lend themselves to reasonably realistic animations, though, like a boy flying a kite and a man flying a control-line model airplane.

GO FLY A KITE!

A person flying a kite is one of the easiest forms of animation to accomplish. The kite appears to be floating in the air, but in reality is supported by a curved wire.

To animate the kite I use a small fan mounted in the ceiling. This causes the kite to bob and weave in a somewhat periodic fashion. The viewer himself modifies this pattern of motion unwittingly, as shown in fig. 1, when he places himself between the fan and the kite. As he shifts position he changes the air pattern reaching the kite.

If you don't want to depend on visitors to modify the kite's flying pattern, use either an oscillating fan or a slowly rotating, irregularly shaped pattern blocking the wind stream, as shown in fig. 2.

And as long as we're talking fans, how about using them to animate windmills or rustle clothes hanging on a wash line?

KITE CONSTRUCTION

Picking the correct wire size is the most crucial part of constructing the kite. For my N scale kite I used a 7½″ length of Detail Associates .010″ brass wire, yielding a string 100 scale feet long. If you would like an 80- to 100-foot string in HO scale, try Detail Associates .015″ wire. For S and O, try K&S .015″ music wire.

Curve the wire by pulling it through the thumb and forefinger of your right hand while slowly rotating it away from your left.

You could make the kite from paper and cement it to the wire, but I have found that method too flimsy. Instead I cut the kite from .002″ brass shim stock and tin it lightly with solder on one side. Then I tin the last ¹⁄₁₆″ of the wire and solder the kite to it. See fig. 3.

You can either cement the other end of the wire to the figure's hand or bend the end of the wire, thread it through a hole drilled in the hand, and fix it in a hole in the ground, as shown in fig. 4.

Fig. 1

Observer randomly programs movement of the kite by changing the pattern of air currents

Fig. 2

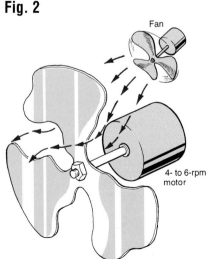

4- to 6-rpm motor

Irregularly shaped rotary wind block programs the air stream, animating the kite

Fig. 3

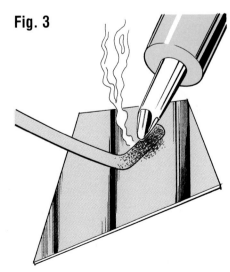

Use a small-tipped soldering iron to sweat solder the brass kite to the .010″-dia. brass kite wire

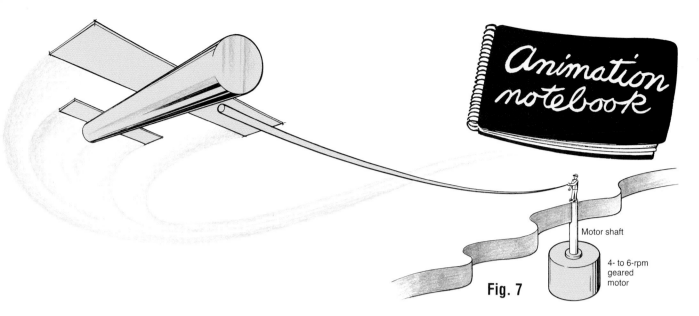

Motor shaft

4- to 6-rpm geared motor

Fig. 7

THE AIRPLANE

Obviously, a miniature man standing on the end of a rotating gear motor shaft does not entirely mimic his real-life counterpart — his feet don't move! This fact, though, is hardly noticeable one foot from the edge of the layout in N scale and two feet from the edge of the layout in HO.

The most difficult part of this animated scene is the airplane itself. In devising a means of fabricating such a tiny model, I remembered the advice of modelers who built fine detail parts for their brass locomotives: "If you can see it and hold it, you can build it." After some thought, I came up with this procedure.

Place a 3″ x 3″ sheet of .002″ brass on a hard, smooth surface such as steel or glass. Lay a steel ruler on the brass close to the edge, and scribe along the edge of the ruler with a no. 10 X-acto blade until the blade cuts through. Remove and discard this strip of brass.

Move the rule .03″ from the newly cut edge, and cut off a parallel strip to

be saved. Now cut a strip .025″ wide. These two strips will become the wings and horizontal stabilizers respectively.

Carefully lay these out on a smooth scrap piece of pine .035″ apart and parallel to each other. Secure the ends with tape, and lightly tin the centers for about ¼″ length.

Next tin about an inch of a 2″ length of .025″-diameter brass rod. Lay the rod perpendicular to the two strips and solder it (see fig. 5). This is your fuselage.

Cut off the left wing ³⁄₃₂″ from the center of the rod, but don't cut off the right wing yet. Tin about the last ¼″ of a piece of .010″ brass wire 4″ long. Then slide it under the left wing almost to the .025″-diameter wire. This is the tether that will go from the plane's wing to the man's hand. See fig. 6.

Now it's true that two lines are actually used to control such a plane, but in N scale this discrepancy is hardly noticed. In scales larger than HO, solder two wires to the wing.

Remove the tape from the assembly, and cut the right wing to the same

length as the left. I would recommend using manicure scissors to do this. Next, you should cut the horizontal stabilizers to length.

Trim the fuselage fore and aft. You are now the proud owner of a rudderless N scale model airplane.

To make the models in Z, HO, S, and O multiply the dimensions for N by .75, 2, 2.5, and 3, respectively. You'll probably want to cement a vertical stabilizer (rudder) to the tail for scales larger than HO.

Hold the other end of the tether about ½″ from the end, heat it to cherry red, and insert it in the hand and arm of the miniature figure. The figure is ready to cement to the shaft of a 4- to 6-rpm Hankscraft or Haydon clock motor. For finishing touches treat the tether wire with Hobby Black and paint the plane a bright color.

Record the sound of a model airplane in flight on a continuous loop tape, and you'll have a credible animated display. Here's hoping these two projects will help you "get things moving" on your model railroad. ✿

Fig. 4

Fig. 5

Fig. 6

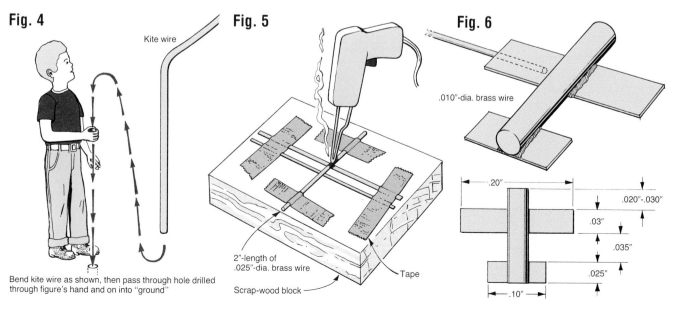

Kite wire

Bend kite wire as shown, then pass through hole drilled through figure's hand and on into "ground"

2″-length of .025″-dia. brass wire

Scrap-wood block

Tape

.010″-dia. brass wire

.20″

.020″-.030″

.03″

.035″

.025″

.10″

An operating windmill

An animated device for N and HO scales

BY RODGER GREDVIG
PHOTOS BY THE AUTHOR

EVERYONE enjoys animated scenes on a model railroad. For many of us this began with Lionel and other toy trains that had smoking locomotives, log dumping cars, rolling oil barrels, operating highway crossing gates, and rockets launched from freight cars.

I've always found such action fascinating, and in an effort to create a little action on my Ntrak module I decided to see if I could develop a simple working windmill. My "pilot model" was suitable for HO, but after that I was able to make a smaller version that looks good in N scale.

PILOT MODEL

For my first attempt I used parts from Campbell HO kit no. 1604. I discarded the kit's tower and constructed a smaller structure from Plastruct A-3 ³/₃₂″ angles, with .030″-square styrene strip for the diagonal bracing.

I filed down the cast ring located about midway out on the fan blades to reduce its bulk. Next I filed down the drive shaft to allow free movement of the fan, and cut down the size of the vane. See figs. 1a and 2. Position the fan on the drive shaft, and carefully form a small mushroom-shaped cap on the shaft end with a soldering iron. Make sure the fan spins freely.

FINAL VERSION

The HO conversion was a bit large for N so I developed a much smaller version from some spoked sequin material. I trimmed the blades on two sequins to make them a scale 8′-0″ in diameter and fastened them as an overlay separated by a wire ring, with the blades staggered. The ring was made by wrapping 24-gauge copper wire around a AAA battery. See figs. 1b and 2. Because of its light mass this model doesn't operate as smoothly as the Campbell one; still, its proportions are better for N scale.

For the fan shaft I used a straight pin cemented into a simulated gearbox housing (made with layers of .020″ styrene that were cut and filed to shape). The

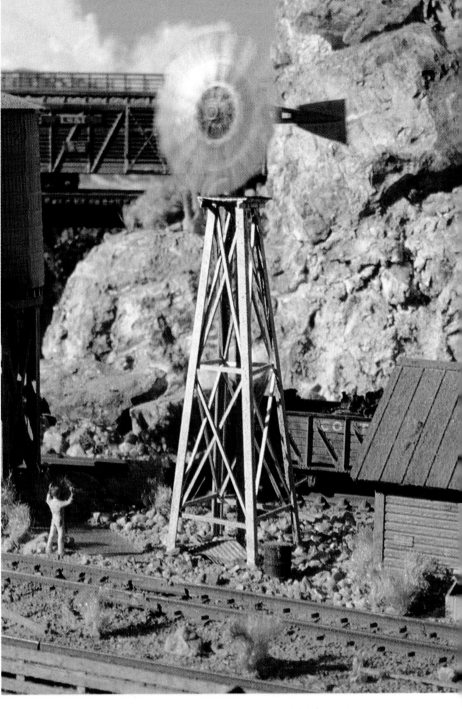

Providing motion to an otherwise static scene, the author's scratchbuilt windmill appears to be pumping water for an adjacent railroad water tank. The figure is checking the fan's operation.

construction of the gearbox and the directional vane is shown in fig. 1b. Fashion and cement a .062″-diameter circle of .010″ styrene to the fan as a bearing hub.

I considered making a more delicate tower using .025″-diameter styrene rod. However, the sturdy nature of the original design used with the Campbell fan proved to be the best choice for the windmill on my traveling Ntrak module.

DRIVE UNIT

After discovering that vibration will cause the fan to spin, I developed a suitable drive system using an aquarium pump. Cut a length of plastic tube from a cotton swab and wrap a few turns around it. See fig. 1a. Drill a hole in the layout base to provide a snug fit around the tape. Attach a small plastic wall anchor to the pump diaphragm with epoxy, as shown in figs. 1a and 3. The pump is mounted under the layout with wood screws, separated from the wood by rubber grommets to reduce vibration, and centered under the hole drilled in the plywood base.

The drive shaft to the fan assembly is a length of ¹/₁₆″ Plastruct tube (actually a tube with a wire center) with the top

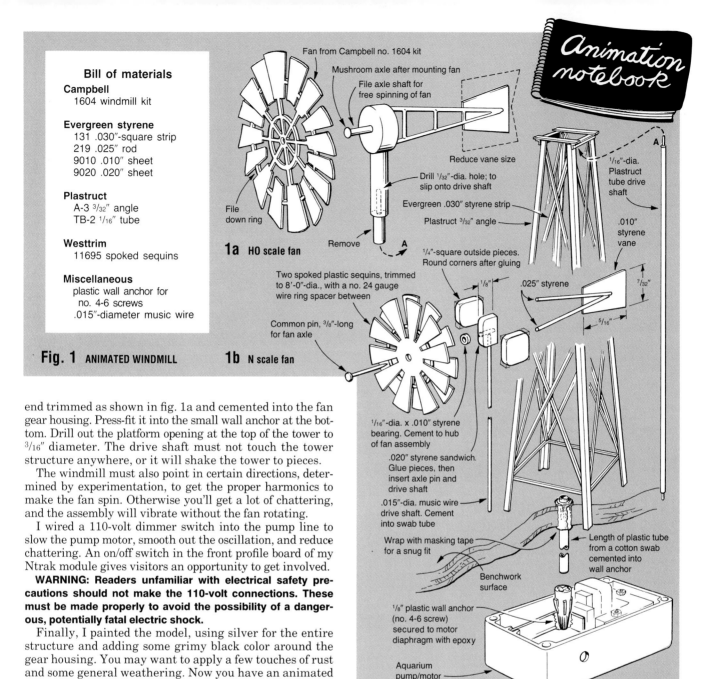

Bill of materials

Campbell
1604 windmill kit

Evergreen styrene
131 .030"-square strip
219 .025" rod
9010 .010" sheet
9020 .020" sheet

Plastruct
A-3 3/32" angle
TB-2 1/16" tube

Westtrim
11695 spoked sequins

Miscellaneous
plastic wall anchor for
no. 4-6 screws
.015"-diameter music wire

Fan from Campbell no. 1604 kit

Mushroom axle after mounting fan

File axle shaft for free spinning of fan

Reduce vane size

File down ring

Remove

Drill 1/32"-dia. hole; to slip onto drive shaft

Evergreen .030" styrene strip

Plastruct 3/32" angle

1a HO scale fan

1/16"-dia. Plastruct tube drive shaft

.010" styrene vane

1/4"-square outside pieces. Round corners after gluing

.025" styrene

Two spoked plastic sequins, trimmed to 8'-0"-dia., with a no. 24 gauge wire ring spacer between

Common pin, 3/8"-long for fan axle

Fig. 1 ANIMATED WINDMILL

1b N scale fan

1/16"-dia. x .010" styrene bearing. Cement to hub of fan assembly

.020" styrene sandwich. Glue pieces, then insert axle pin and drive shaft

.015"-dia. music wire drive shaft. Cement into swab tube

Wrap with masking tape for a snug fit

Benchwork surface

Length of plastic tube from a cotton swab cemented into wall anchor

1/8" plastic wall anchor (no. 4-6 screw) secured to motor diaphragm with epoxy

Aquarium pump/motor

Not to scale

end trimmed as shown in fig. 1a and cemented into the fan gear housing. Press-fit it into the small wall anchor at the bottom. Drill out the platform opening at the top of the tower to 3/16" diameter. The drive shaft must not touch the tower structure anywhere, or it will shake the tower to pieces.

The windmill must also point in certain directions, determined by experimentation, to get the proper harmonics to make the fan spin. Otherwise you'll get a lot of chattering, and the assembly will vibrate without the fan rotating.

I wired a 110-volt dimmer switch into the pump line to slow the pump motor, smooth out the oscillation, and reduce chattering. An on/off switch in the front profile board of my Ntrak module gives visitors an opportunity to get involved.

WARNING: Readers unfamiliar with electrical safety precautions should not make the 110-volt connections. These must be made properly to avoid the possibility of a dangerous, potentially fatal electric shock.

Finally, I painted the model, using silver for the entire structure and adding some grimy black color around the gear housing. You may want to apply a few touches of rust and some general weathering. Now you have an animated attraction to fascinate yet another generation of impressionable modelers. ◌

Fig. 2. This view shows the two versions of the fan assembly. On the right, the one with the reworked Campbell kit fan works better, but it's a bit large for N scale. The one at the left uses spoked sequins.

Fig. 3. Vibration provided by an aquarium pump makes the fan turn. A small plastic wall anchor is attached to the diaphragm with epoxy. The plastic tube stuck into it carries the motion to the fan assembly.

The streets and sidewalks on the author's HO scale West Hoosic Division of the B&M look like concrete, but they're really styrene. Lou's layout was featured in the July 1988 MR.

Concrete streets from styrene sheets

As simple as cut, scribe, and glue

BY LOU SASSI
PHOTOS BY THE AUTHOR

I CAN REMEMBER, back in my childhood days, riding to Lake George, N. Y., on old Rt. 9 for a day of boating. The trip is as vivid in my memory as if it were yesterday — the car tires thumping across the seams in the concrete pavement.

Since my HO scale West Hoosic Division of the Boston & Maine is set sometime around 1950, I thought a similar concrete paved thoroughfare would be appropriate for the layout. After some experimentation, I discovered it was possible to create the look of concrete pavement in HO by using styrene plastic sheets and strips that are manufactured by Evergreen Scale Models.

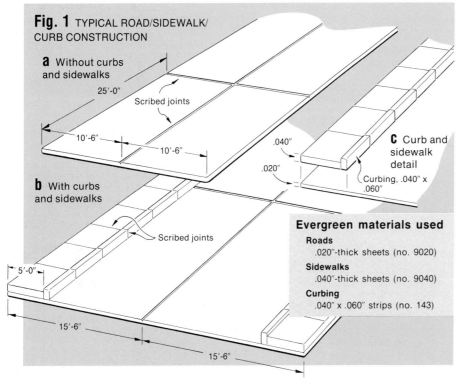

Fig. 1 TYPICAL ROAD/SIDEWALK/CURB CONSTRUCTION

a Without curbs and sidewalks

25'-0"

Scribed joints

10'-6"   10'-6"

.040"

.020"

c Curb and sidewalk detail

Curbing, .040" x .060"

b With curbs and sidewalks

Scribed joints

5'-0"

15'-6"

15'-6"

Evergreen materials used

Roads
.020"-thick sheets (no. 9020)

Sidewalks
.040"-thick sheets (no. 9040)

Curbing
.040" x .060" strips (no. 143)

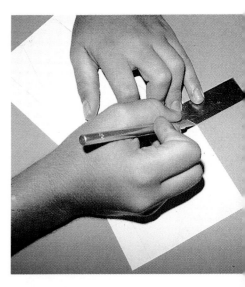

Fig. 2. The author demonstrates the proper way to scribe styrene with the back of the tip of a hobby-knife blade. To represent separating strips between concrete slabs, he simply makes one or two passes. To remove excess material, he makes several passes and then snaps off the excess.

PROTOTYPE ROADS AND SIDEWALKS

Using the prototype highway as an example, I first established the width and length of each concrete slab at 10½ x 25 feet. This gives an overall road width (two slabs placed side by side) of 21 feet. Figure 1a illustrates typical rural highway construction.

For urban areas that require sidewalks, I have added an extra 5 feet on each side of the road slabs to serve as a base for the sidewalks and curbs. Each sidewalk slab measures 2½ x 5 feet in length. Figures 1b and 1c illustrate curb and sidewalk configurations.

MODEL HIGHWAYS AND BYWAYS

The seams that create each road and walk slab are first laid out on the styrene sheets with a pencil and scale rule and then scribed with a no. 11 X-acto knife (fig. 2). The trick when scribing is to use the back of the point, dragging the blade upside down alongside the straightedge. The seams in the curbing and sidewalk are made in the same manner. When removing excess stock from your sheets, simply scribe with your knife and snap off that material.

Figure 3 illustrates a typical right-angle street intersection. Note that two of the intersecting streets will meet in the center. A line should be scribed at the butt joint after the cement has dried. The other two streets will meet on the edges of the two intersecting streets. These two should have end slabs only 12½ feet long, not the full-length 25 feet. The butt-joint seams should not be visible when cemented and painted. The sidewalks have a 5-foot-radius piece at each corner.

GLUING TIPS

Once the components are scribed and separated, test-fit everything — glue nothing. Be sure that the surface the

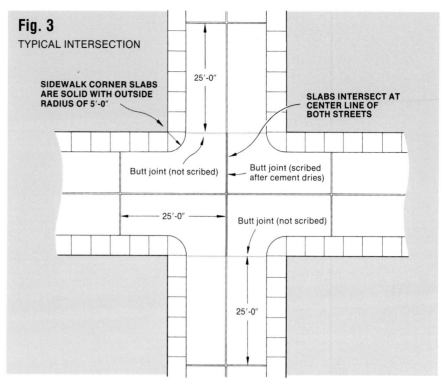

Fig. 3
TYPICAL INTERSECTION

SIDEWALK CORNER SLABS ARE SOLID WITH OUTSIDE RADIUS OF 5'-0"

25'-0"

SLABS INTERSECT AT CENTER LINE OF BOTH STREETS

Butt joint (not scribed)

Butt joint (scribed after cement dries)

25'-0"

Butt joint (not scribed)

25'-0"

road is applied to is as smooth and flat as possible. When you're sure everything is right, begin gluing the road sheets to the layout base. The sidewalk and curbing are glued to the road sheets after the road is in place.

There is a trick to gluing the road to its base and the road and sidewalk to each other. Do not use a solvent-type cement on the entire underside of either the road or sidewalks. The lack of air circulation will not allow proper drying of such an adhesive, and eventually it may eat through the styrene and turn the sidewalk or road into a sticky morass. (This is undesirable unless you're modeling wet cement or melted asphalt!)

I use white glue on the broad, flat surfaces; then I run just a thin bead of

plastic cement along the edges. The curbing can be secured with solvent cement with no problems. If necessary, place some weights on the road surface until it has dried thoroughly.

COLORING

Once a segment of road is in place, I airbrush it with a mix of 3 parts Floquil Reefer White to 1 part Floquil Concrete. When this has dried, black and raw umber dry colors (I use Winsor and Newton) are rubbed on with a soft cloth to represent dirt and oil deposits.

Now that your HO scale people have good roads to travel, they won't have to worry about the wear and tear on their autos. Remember, those are vintage vehicles they're driving. ☼

Working streetlights

In a few evenings you can make enough to light up your model towns

BY EARL SMALLSHAW

ONCE OUR MODEL railroads reach a level of completeness, we look for ways to enhance our scenery and structures. A natural extension of model scenery is interior lighting of structures to create night scenes. After all, prototype railroads operate both day and night.

Unfortunately, the next step, exterior lighting, is often overlooked. Yet streetlights are commonplace — from the smallest towns to the largest cities.

Reasons for excluding streetlights range from cost (particularly if you need many) to appearance. Most commercial streetlights are oversize, especially in the smaller scales. Those that are close to

scale, don't light. In both cases, each streetlight can cost several dollars.

Happily, there is a compromise. Campbell produces a package of three lantern-type streetlights for $2.00. They're very close to scale and can easily be modified to light. This type of light is obviously more typical of earlier periods, though many can still be found in cities as large as Boston. In any event, the technique for modifying these streetlights can be adapted to other, more modern lamps.

The total cost of each modified light comes to about $2.10:
Lamp — 66 cents (Campbell, 3 for $2.00)
Bulb (12-14 volts) — $1.39 (NJ International)
Brass tubing — 5 cents
Even if you plan to illuminate a metropolis, $2.10 is easier to bear than

This modified Campbell streetlamp adds an extra touch of realism to this city scene on the author's HO scale Middletown & Mystic Mines Ry.

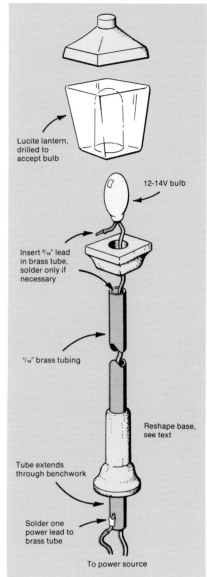

Lucite lantern, drilled to accept bulb

12-14V bulb

Insert ³/₁₆″ lead in brass tube, solder only if necessary

¹/₁₆″ brass tubing

Reshape base, see text

Tube extends through benchwork

Solder one power lead to brass tube

To power source

$4.95, which is the average price of a commercial unit.

Begin by removing the pole portion of the lamppost, from the top of the base to just under the base of the lantern. Remove any flash from the bottom of the base so that it remains perpendicular and steady for the drilling process. Drill a ¹/₁₆″ hole in the base, making sure that the hole is both centered and perpendicular. If drilled correctly, the hole will exit through the exact center of the base. A drill press makes the job easier, although careful hand drilling is possible.

Once you're satisfied with the hole, insert a 1⁷/₈″ length of ¹/₁₆″ brass tubing into the base, allowing about ½″ to protrude from the bottom. This helps to mount your streetlight and ensures that it won't be knocked over, destroying your electrical connection.

Realizing that these streetlights were meant to stand on their own convinced me that the diameter of the base was too large. To reduce it I chucked the ¹/₁₆″ tubing, with the base attached, in my drill press. As it turned, I held a single-edged razor blade against the base until it was reduced to about 1½ scale feet. Filing blended the new diameter to the base contour.

The base of the lantern also has a ¹/₁₆″ hole drilled through the center. Slip the base over the top end of the ¹/₁₆″ tubing flush with the end.

Carefully separate the leads to the grain-of-wheat bulb as close to the bulb as possible. Don't get too close and break the connection. Cut one lead to about ³/₁₆″ from the bulb, then carefully scrape it with your razor blade to remove any insulating lacquer.

Now thread the uncut lead through the ¹/₁₆″ tubing. The short lead is bent inward, so as to enter and press against the inside of the tubing. This lead can be soldered to the tubing, but I found that the pressure of the wire inside the tubing was enough for positive electrical contact. If you do solder it, be careful that the heat from the soldering iron doesn't harm the bulb.

Next, drill the clear Lucite lantern through the center so it can accept the bulb. The size of this drill will vary depending on the diameter of the bulb. The hole must, however, be just big enough to allow the bulb to clear.

You may find that the tip of the bulb protrudes from the top. If so, the cap of the lantern must be drilled with a relief hole to accept the tip of the bulb. Be careful not to drill completely through the cap. Mounting the bulb as close as possible to the ¹/₁₆″ tubing will minimize the depth of the clearance hole required.

Before you permanently assemble the lamp, solder an additional wire lead to the side of the ¹/₁₆″ tubing where it protrudes from the base. Connect this new lead and the bulb lead (threaded through the tube) to an AC/DC power source not exceeding 12 volts. If it lights, you're ready to proceed. Otherwise, touch one power lead to the ³/₁₆″ lead of the bulb. If it lights, your connection to the inside of the ¹/₁₆″ tubing must be made more positive. Soldering may be the only solution. If the bulb still doesn't light, it's defective and needs replacing.

Once you're sure everything is okay, assemble the lamp using your favorite adhesive. As the glue is drying, test the bulb again. It's easier to correct any problem before the glue sets.

I painted my lamppost with Floquil's Grimy Black. Then I painted the edges of the lantern to simulate the frame.

To install a working streetlight, drill a vertical ¹/₈″ hole through the bench top and insert it. If it leans at all, either the hole you drilled is not vertical or the lamppost is not perpendicular to the bottom of the base. A larger hole can be drilled, if necessary, making sure the hole size doesn't exceed the diameter of the base.

If the base isn't square with the post, scrape away at the bottom of the base with an X-acto knife until you've corrected the problem.

Although each lamp is rated at 12 volts, I power mine at about 8 volts. I have three streetlights wired in series to a 25-volt power supply. Each light receives a bit more than 8 volts. This lower voltage not only prolongs the life of the bulbs, but the slightly dimmer light looks better. We don't want the streetlights to overpower the scene, just enhance it.

It takes only about an hour to modify each Campbell light. In a few evenings you'll have enough to illuminate the streets of almost any city. Then wait for visiting model railroaders to ask again and again, "How did you *do that?*" ✿

Fig. 1. Rutland Ry. RS-3 no. 207 is busy shuttling a Boston & Maine boxcar as it crosses this blacktop highway on Lou's HO scale West Hoosic Division (featured in our July 1988 issue).

Three for the road

Grade crossings for three types of roads

Fig. 2. Above: The author uses a slightly different technique where dirt roads cross the tracks. **Fig. 3. Below:** Follow his suggestions, and you'll find that it isn't difficult to build impressive grade crossings like this one on Route 2 (concrete highway).

BY LOU SASSI
PHOTOS BY THE AUTHOR

ONCE THE highways and byways on my HO scale Boston & Maine West Hoosic Division began meandering through the countryside, it soon became apparent to the railroad's "B&B" (bridges and buildings) gangs that they must provide proper grade crossings where necessary. To date they have constructed three types.

In fig. 1 the blacktop road crosses the tracks on wooden planks. Actually, these "planks" are from a sheet of Kappler Mill & Lumber Co. scribed "V" basswood with scale 6"-wide boards.

The dirt road in fig. 2 crosses on Kappler scale 8 x 8-foot planks that are glued on each side of both rails and backfilled with sand.

Figure 3 shows a concrete road crossing the tracks over a wood plank grade crossing much like the one in fig. 1. This one, however, is made of individual scale 2 x 8-foot Kappler wood strips.

In all three examples I have begun by staining the wood with a mixture that's 20 percent Floquil Grimy Black and 80 percent Dio-Sol. Then I secured the pieces in place with Duco Cement using an NMRA track gauge to make sure the trains' flanges passed between the inside of each running rail and the wood crossing.

The height of the wooden members must be below that of the rails by about a scale 2" to 3"; otherwise, the locomotive wheels ride up on the planks and lose electrical contact or possibly derail. I use code 70 rail, so I didn't need any spacers to bring my planks close to rail height. If you have code 83 or 100 rail, you may want to use scale lumber with a larger vertical dimension. Another option would be to cut some wood spacers, glue them to the ties, and lay your crossing stock on them (fig. 4).

That's about all there is to it. I hope you will be able to incorporate one or two of these grade crossings in your own pike. I'm sure your HO scale motorists will appreciate the effort! ☼

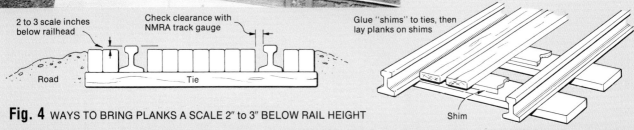

2 to 3 scale inches below railhead

Check clearance with NMRA track gauge

Road

Tie

Glue "shims" to ties, then lay planks on shims

Shim

Fig. 4 WAYS TO BRING PLANKS A SCALE 2" to 3" BELOW RAIL HEIGHT

Building better abutments

BY ROBERT SMAUS
PHOTOS BY THE AUTHOR

AFTER CAREFULLY ASSEMBLING several bridge kits, I wanted to make sure they sat on equally fine abutments, the winged type so common along the Southern Pacific right-of-way on my Los Angeles Division. I first thought of casting the front and wings as separate pieces and then fitting them together, but I've never been very good at miter cuts, so I developed the method shown here.

Briefly, here's the idea. After casting the front face of the abutment, I tilt it up in the same mold and, one after the other, I cast the wings onto it. Plaster bonds tightly to plaster if both pieces are damp.

To back up a little, I wanted the abutments to look as though they were cast about 1920, when the concrete was poured into forms made of individual boards. To get that look, I first cut grooves with a hobby knife into a piece of plywood. See fig. 1. These cuts would represent the concrete that oozed from

Fig. 1. Left. Using a straightedge as a guide, make shallow cuts into a piece of plywood. These represent individual boards used in forms in the 1920s. A few crosswise cuts indicate board ends. Fig. 2. Above. The rest of the form is scrap wood tacked in place. The extra piece inside is for a ledge for the bridge to rest on. Wait until the plaster is warm before removing the abutment. Fig. 3. Above. In preparation for forming the wings, first tape a piece of aluminum foil in place on the plywood. Then rub a toothbrush across it to pick up the grooves of the plywood. The foil serves as a release agent for the plaster.

between the form boards. I also roughed up the plywood with a saw and the hobby knife. Construction companies used the cheapest of lumber, and the grain left its imprint.

This plywood base would be used over and over again, actually getting more character with each use. (I even used it as a form for bridge sides, culverts, and tunnel portals.) The other sides of the mold were made from scrap pieces of wood tacked in place, as shown in fig. 2.

Since you are custom fitting the abutments to the bridge, you can make a realistic ledge for the bridge to rest on, also shown in fig. 2.

Pour the plaster, mixed to about the consistency of pancake batter, directly into the mold. A few sharp raps against the workbench will settle it and send the bubbles to the surface. When the plaster has set up and is warm to the touch (about 20 minutes), remove the temporary sides of the mold. Then tap the abutment out of the mold. It is very important to make sure the plaster is warm before removing it from the mold; any sooner and it may crumble; much later and it will stick. Immediately, clean up the mold with a wire brush.

Now, for the wings. Lay a piece of aluminum foil over the plywood base and with a toothbrush rub until the foil takes the shape of the grooves. See fig. 3.

Now prop up the face of the abutment (fig. 4) at the desired angle and add scrap pieces of wood to complete the form for the wing. Pour the plaster, being sure it joins the face of the abutment. You may wish to pick up the face of the abutment a little to make sure plaster gets into this gap, but then press it down tightly against the plywood base. Any plaster that squeezes out in the process is easily trimmed off later.

When the plaster has become warm to the touch, lift the abutment from the mold (the tinfoil makes this possible). Clean off any excess plaster from the abutment by scraping it away with a hobby knife.

Figure 6 demonstrates an interesting variation on this method: To make a four-sided concrete pier to go between the abutments, first cast the pier on the same piece of plywood, then "print" the other three sides on it by pressing them into shallow puddles of plaster poured on top of the foil. After the plaster has set up, simply trim off the excess and repeat the process on the other sides. The result is a pier that looks like it was poured into a four-sided mold.

When the plaster is dry (several days later), paint it with a mix of Floquil Concrete and Reefer White, add streaks of rust running down from the bridge shoes with pastel chalks, and if you are modeling Los Angeles, add the necessary graffiti. ✿

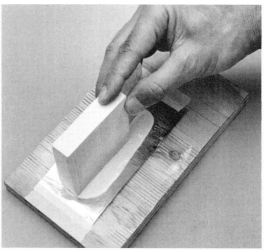

Fig. 4. Left. Tilt the abutment at the desired angle, and form the rest of the mold with scrap wood. Now fill it with plaster, being sure to force the plaster into the gap under the abutment where the faces meet. Fig. 5. Above. Any plaster that oozes out of the forms is easily trimmed off by scraping it with the flat edge of a hobby knife. If the wing is too thick, it's easy to trim with a hacksaw. Fig. 6. Above. Freestanding pier. First cast the basic shape, then "print" the other three sides by holding them in very shallow puddles of plaster until it sets (about 20 minutes). Clean up excess with a hobby knife.

Light up the night with NEON

Fig. 1. UV LAMPS. "Black lights" are available in many sizes. The black tubes are designated "BLB," and the white one is designated "BL." Since BL tubes also emit visible light, only BLB lamps are usable for modeling. Commercial black light sources, like the one at left, are *not* recommended because they produce harmful short-wave UV light as well as the harmless long-wave light produced by the BLB lamps.

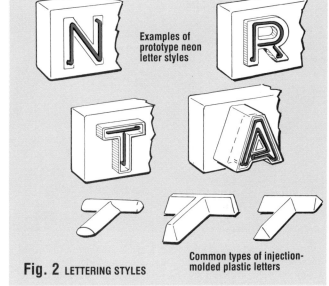

Examples of prototype neon letter styles

Common types of injection-molded plastic letters

Fig. 2 LETTERING STYLES

"Neon" signs, colored with fluorescent paint and lit by ultraviolet black light, add life to nighttime scenes.

Using fluorescent paint and black light to model neon signs

BY D. DEREK VERNER
PHOTOS BY THE AUTHOR

NEON SIGNS are familiar sights in every city and town. From the sputtering "EATS" sign flickering in the darkness alongside a desolate stretch of highway to the gaudy "Strip" in Las Vegas, neon signs have become a traditional part of our landscape. They go back further than you might think, as they were introduced in 1910.

Prototype neon signs consist of glass tubing, 1/4" to 5/8" in diameter, bent to shape and filled with neon or mixtures of other rare gasses at reduced pressure. Electrodes at the ends of each section of tubing are connected to a high-voltage transformer, which causes the gasses to ionize and give off light. The color of the light is a function of the choice of gasses and color and coating of the tubing.

MODELING NEON SIGNS

The best and least expensive way to capture the effect of neon is by using fluorescent paint illuminated by ultraviolet (UV) light. "Black light" lamps like the ones shown in fig. 1 are available from large electrical supply dealers and range in size from a 48", 40-watt unit to a 5¼", 4-watt unit. They operate in a manner similar to fluorescent lamps.

Fixtures for these tubes differ in only one respect from any other fluorescent fixture: The reflector is chrome-plated instead of painted white. The shiny surface redirects UV light from the back side so that it isn't wasted. A painted surface will absorb most of this light. Simply covering the reflector with aluminum duct tape or aluminum foil (shiny side out) will work fine.

Fluorescent paint is available in a wide range of colors. It's sold in craft, hobby, and hardware stores in both spray cans and bottles. I used Testor's fluorescent model paints for most of the signs in the photos. This type of paint appears very bright because it reacts to the UV light present in most light sources. For modeling purposes it makes our signs appear lit even in daylight scenes without UV lamps.

SOURCES FOR LETTERING

Except for small window signs and some skeleton roof signs, most neon signs follow one of the forms shown in fig. 2. This is because businesses want the sign to be visible in daylight as well as at night, when the real impact of neon signs comes across.

At first, the logical way to form model signs appears to be to shape them from thin wire. However, several attempts to do that produced results that I felt were less than successful. The lower "Crown Hotel" sign in fig. 3 shows the results. It's very difficult to form properly proportioned letters by hand. An ideal solution (manufacturers take note) would be to have signs photoetched from suitable artwork.

Using small plastic letters is much easier. Acrylic letters in several colors are available from plastic supply stores. Cast-metal letters are generally not as suitable because they cannot be cemented with plastic solvent.

Several plastic structure kits made for the international market have usable letters. The "Pace Freight," "Wonder Bar," and "Chicago Fruit" signs in fig. 3 came from signs supplied with such kits. Since they're sold in many countries, they frequently include the same words in several languages, offering anagram and Scrabble fans a challenge to see what English words can be made from the letters supplied.

Injection-molded plastic letters usually have one of the three cross sections shown in fig. 2. For modeling, the best shape is the truncated triangle. This is because, in order to mimic the prototype sign formats and reduce the width of the letter strokes, we will light up only the narrow front surface of the letters. Letters with a curved cross section are the least suitable, as they require the entire letter to be illuminated. However, they can be used to model the type of illuminated sign that uses vacuum-formed letters lit from behind by fluorescent tubes.

Letters with a triangular cross section can be used, but it's difficult to paint the sharp front edge. To do this, pour a small puddle of paint on a sheet of glass and dip the letter in so that only the front touches the paint. Another method is to use a fluorescent marking pen, such as the one shown at the upper left of fig. 3. These pens are

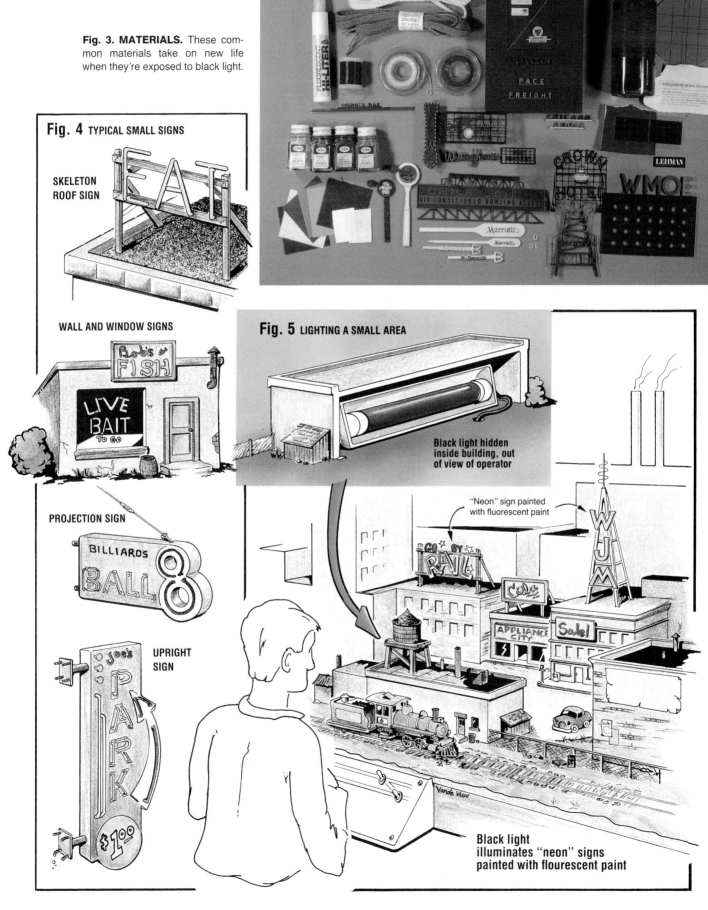

Fig. 3. MATERIALS. These common materials take on new life when they're exposed to black light.

Fig. 4 TYPICAL SMALL SIGNS

SKELETON ROOF SIGN

WALL AND WINDOW SIGNS

PROJECTION SIGN

UPRIGHT SIGN

Fig. 5 LIGHTING A SMALL AREA

Black light hidden inside building, out of view of operator

"Neon" sign painted with fluorescent paint

Black light illuminates "neon" signs painted with flourescent paint

46

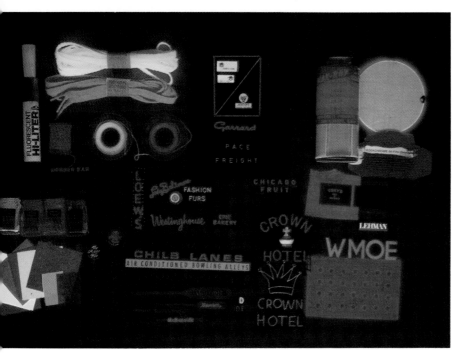

easier to control than a brush and can coat the sharp edge with ease.

For fluorescent paints to light up brightly they *must* be applied over a white surface. If the letters are in another color, the area where the fluorescent paint will be applied should first be painted flat white.

Keep your eyes open for swizzle sticks, condiment forks, nameplates, and other items with bas-relief or three-dimensional letters. The "Magic Pan," "Westinghouse," "Garrard," "McDonald's," "Marriott," and "Lady Baltimore" signs in fig. 3 are from such sources.

Figure 4 shows several typical sign designs. Skeleton roof signs generally have some sort of grid or framework to which the sign is affixed. The "Lady Baltimore" sign in fig. 3 was mounted on a Grandt Line window casting, and the hand-formed "Crown Hotel" sign was mounted on a frame made from Plastruct angle pieces. The other "Crown Hotel" sign is mounted on a piece of wire screen. The solder blobs at the intersections of the wires can be filed down, if they seem objectionable.

Letters mounted against a wall, such as "Lulu's Lunchroom" and "Lacy's Variety" are simply cemented to an appropriately colored background, as are the projection and upright sign letters.

OTHER MATERIALS

Fluorescent paper, shown in fig. 3, is available from art supply stores. The paper can be used as glowing backgrounds for signs in which the lettering is done with black dry-transfer letters. That's how the lower half of the "Chilb Lanes" bowling alley sign was done.

One way to make window and other signs is to use the paper (or the paint)

behind a Kodalith negative, like the "Tony's Fruits and Vegetables" and "Lehman" signs in fig. 3. (The high-contrast Kodalith film is available from large photography stores; professional photographers or graphic artists can also shoot these from your prepared artwork.)

Make sure the paper is in tight contact with the negative, or this technique won't work properly. Place small dots of Walthers Goo or contact cement on the opaque areas of the negative to bind it closely to the paper.

Decals can be mounted on fluorescent paper if the decal carrier film is the full size of the backing paper. Decals not made this way won't work well because the edge of the decal film will be visible. The "Lorie's Gifts" sign illustrates this method. Before applying the decal, spray the paper with a sealant such as Testor's Glosscote.

Many art supply stores carry fluorescent dry-transfer letters. The upper half of the "Chilb Lanes" sign was made using these. Even though the letters have an under-printing of white pigment, they work better if mounted on a light but contrasting color background rather than the dark one shown. Note that this sign is supposedly frontlit by floodlights. This technique works as well for signs supposedly backlit.

Another way of modeling a sign lit by floodlights is to use a transparent liquid called Living Light. Figure 3 shows this product next to a film box that's been given a coat of it. Notice that the painted area lights up brightly and the printed lettering shows through. Living Light can be applied to any surface, causing it to light up under UV light. It can be used for signs or to create

puddles of light around dummy streetlights. Living Light (stock no. A-810) is distributed by Ultra-Violet Products, San Gabriel, CA 91776.

Ordinary paper, including many signs offered by model suppliers, is sometimes fluorescent without special treatment. Two rectangles of typing paper are shown on top of the color swatches in fig. 3. One glows brightly under UV, the other does not. That's because manufacturers often put fluorescent dyes into products to make them appear whiter and brighter.

You may be surprised at how many products around the house glow under the influence of UV light. This can be a drawback if you use UV lighting on your layout. You may find that some of your modeling materials glow brightly when you don't want them to. If this happens, you may have to repaint the item in non-fluorescent paint. Some dealers in UV products market a transparent liquid that will stop the transmission of UV light so the item no longer glows.

Other fluorescent items shown in fig. 3 include elastic, thread, yarn, and shoelaces. All the fluorescent fabric materials I've seen are made of fine filaments that are bundled together. These can be unraveled and regrouped into bundles as thin as you like. They're excellent for modeling straight lengths of neon tubing to outline signs or serve as accent lighting on movie marquees. The lines shown on the piece of construction paper were made this way. Fluorescent drafting tape (as narrow as $1/32''$) is also available.

Some plastics are available in fluorescent colors, and fig. 3 shows some acrylic pieces and molded letters. The letters are rather large for most purposes, but they work well for call letters mounted atop a broadcasting station.

PLACING THE UV LAMPS

If you plan to use fluorescent materials extensively on your layout, you may want to flood an entire scene with UV light by suspending large (40-watt) fixtures overhead. If you do, be sure to take full advantage of the benefits of UV by using the pigments and materials for other lighting effects. How about stars and a glowing moon for your night sky? You could light street lamps, vehicle and train lights, and windows. Even the windows in flat backgrounds can be lighted with paint or small squares of fluorescent paper.

If you want to light only a few signs or areas, the smaller-sized lamps can be concealed within or behind other structures as shown in fig. 5. Remember that these lights operate on 110 volts and should be wired accordingly.

Try some of the techniques outlined in this article. When visitors admire your handiwork, you can be assured that it's a good sign. ⚭

Industrial lighting

How to add outdoor lighting to your layout's business districts

BY ROBERT SMAUS
PHOTOS BY THE AUTHOR

WHEN IT COMES TO LIGHTING a layout, you almost have to make your own fixtures. Though there is a bewildering assortment of bulbs and other electrical paraphernalia out there, there are precious few light fixtures that look like they would be caught anywhere near a railroad.

Campbell Scale Models makes the closest thing — little brass lampshades of distinctly industrial heritage. And they work very neatly with Pacific Fast Mail's microminiature lamp bulbs. There may be other brands that work, but PFM's are the only one I found that slip right into the shades.

These PFM bulbs come in packs of 10, and because they are only 1.8 volts you can't just hook them up to your power pack or they'll burn out in an instant. You'll have to connect all 10 in series or add an appropriate-size resistor in series with each bulb. I'll describe how to figure all that out in the next few paragraphs. Anyone who has even a rudimentary understanding of things electrical can skip ahead to the assembly instructions. Those of us (myself included) who don't know a volt from an amp, must deal with these matters first.

VOLTS, AMPS, OHMS

Hooking all the bulbs together is called wiring in series, connecting one wire of one bulb to one wire of the next bulb, and so on, so they're all joined together like a string of sausages. When you wire in series you can simply add the voltage of each bulb to see what the total is, i.e. — 10 x 1.8 = 18 volts. If you apply 18 volts to this string of series-wired lights, each one will have 1.8 volts applied to it and will operate at full brightness. If you connect this string to the 16VAC accessory terminals of your power pack, each bulb will have 1.6 volts applied to it, which means it won't be quite as bright, but it will last longer.

Wall-mounted fixtures, common over doors and loading platforms, are simple to make.

Resistors can also be used (don't quit on me now!). If you're only going to use a few bulbs, you'll need to wire a resistor into the series of bulbs, somewhere between the first bulb and the power pack, though it can be on either end of the string. Resistors eat up the extra voltage so the bulbs don't get too much and burn out. Resistors are cheap and available at electronics stores, including Radio Shack.

Here's how to figure out what value resistor you need. First, you must find out how many amps each bulb draws. If you have

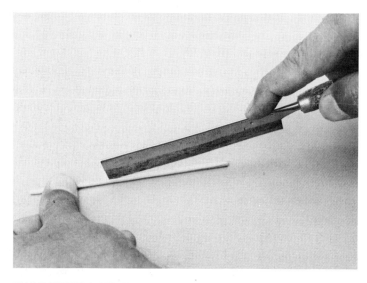

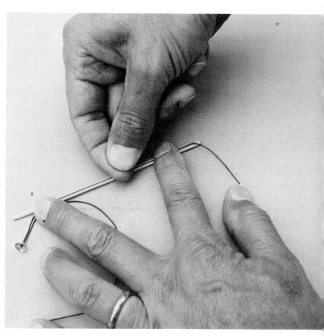

POLE-MOUNTED LIGHT FIXTURE. Step 1. Above. After tapering the top of the dowel, cut a shallow slit down the side with a hobby knife and widen it with a razor saw, as shown. **Step 2. Right.** After cementing on the Campbell shade, use your fingernail to force one of the wires into the slit. If it doesn't fit, widen the slit.

Pole-mounted fixtures require little more than a lamp, a shade, and a dowel.

an ammeter, you can measure it. Fortunately, PFM tells you how much its bulbs draw — 60 milliamps or .060 amp. If you divide that by the voltage, you'll get ohms, which is the measure of resistance. That's called Ohm's Law and the formula is Volts ÷ Amps = Ohms. So, 1.8 volts ÷ .060 amps = 30 ohms. If you didn't follow all of that (My dad, who's an electrical engineer, had to tell it to me three times in three different ways!), just remember the 30 ohms part. This is how much resistance each bulb has.

Now multiply the number of bulbs you have in your string by this 30 ohms and subtract the answer from 200 ohms for a 12-volt supply, or from 266 ohms for a 16-volt supply. The result is how big a resistor you need in series with your bulb or bulbs. If you can't find a resistor exactly that size, opt for the next higher standard value to be on the safe side.

Here's an example: You have 6 PFM bulbs connected in series — 6 x 30 = 180 ohms. You have a 12-volt supply, so the resistor you need equals 200 minus 180, which equals 20 ohms. Since there is no 20-ohm resistor, get the next size up which is 22 ohms.

If you want to run each bulb individually, you'll need a 220-ohm resistor in series with each bulb if using a 12-volt supply, or a 270-ohm resistor if using a 16-volt supply.

The Radio Shack resistors I bought are rated at ½-watt, but if you use less that 5 bulbs from the set, you really need a resistor rated at 1 watt. If you can't find one, simply string two ½-watt resistors together, with each having half the ohms required. For instance, if you need a 220-ohm resistor to run a single bulb, use two 110-ohm resistors wired in series along with the bulb. Their sum will equal the necessary ohms and watts.

INSTALLATION

With the math out of the way, take a look at the bulb leads. Notice how small in diameter the leads are? They are almost the size of scale conduit. They are also wonderfully long — about 7″. This let's you make light fixtures with lightning speed.

To make a wall-mounted industrial fixture, slip a Campbell shade over the wires and onto the bulb. Cement it in place using one of the CA cements that contain a filler (Zap-A-Gap is one brand). Now simply form the wires into the shape desired (usually some gooseneck shape for industrial lighting), hold the two wires together so they are touching, and dab on some CA. Paint the wire black, paint the inside of the shade white and, a few minutes later, paint the outside green.

You can easily make this a pole-mounted fixture by cutting a slit — first with a hobby knife, then with a razor saw — the length of a ⅛″ wood dowel. See the four step-by-step photos. Cram one of the wires into this slit and glue the other on top of it. A single wire on the outside of the pole looks like it could be conduit, which is a believable situation.

Before installing the wire, you can rough up the wood by scraping with the edge of the razor saw. At the top of the pole drill a hole and glue a piece of brass wire between the pole and the lamp shade. Glue the wires above this bracket together. Paint all the wire and the bracket black. Stain the pole with Floquil Maple, then haphazardly paint it Roof Brown, and finally dust on a little black pastel chalk. A piece of brass wire and a couple of Grandt turnbuckles, painted Rust, make a fine guy wire and add another dimension to this pole that would dignify any industrial area on the other side of the tracks. ⚙

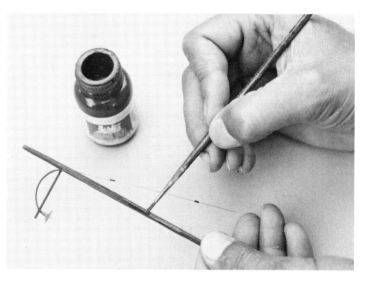

Step 3. Above. Carefully align the two wires at the top, form them into a gooseneck, and cement them together, side-by-side. Next, drill a hole for the brass support and cement it to the lamp. Then cement the second wire on top of the first one and run them down the length of the dowel.

Step 4. Above. Add the brass guy wire and Grandt turnbuckles. Paint them and the brass lamp support Floquil Weathered Black, then brush on some rust (a half-and half mix of Rust and Roof Brown). Paint the electrical wires black, then stain the dowel Maple and brush on Roof Brown.

Harvey Simon created a unique structure by bending the walls of an HO scale Magnuson Models kit.

Cooking up a curved-front building

Hot water is the key to reshaping a Magnuson kit

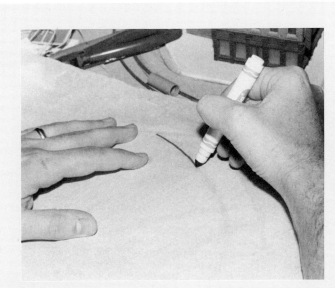

Fig. 1. PLOTTING THE CURVE. Make a template by tracing the outline of the building front from the layout onto a piece of paper.

Fig. 2. DIPPING THE WALL. Submerge half of the wall section in near-boiling water for about 30 seconds to soften it for shaping.

BY HARVEY SIMON
PHOTOS BY THE AUTHOR

M Y FAVORITE PART of the hobby is building structures. Over the past year I've been slowly constructing an HO scale trolley layout, requiring several buildings for an urban setting depicting New England in the 1940s. My challenge has been to make the city look unique while using commercial kits and common components for the structures.

One city block of the layout is curved to conform to the curve of the street tracks. This design was intentional, as I wanted to re-create a scene typical of the era and locale I was modeling. For a truly convincing look, I wanted to feature a masonry building with a curved front that would match the curve of the sidewalk. I knew that the challenging part of building such a model would be to form curves in its walls.

Although I was unaware of a commercial kit featuring a curved front, I did recall reading in a Walthers catalog advertisement that Magnuson's normally brittle wall castings can be curved by first immersing them in hot water. This proved to be the solution to my problem.

To test this idea, I experimented by trying to curve a piece of Magnuson sidewalk left over from an earlier project. Sure enough, when submerged in very hot (near-boiling) water, the piece softened and was easily curved. With this in mind, I decided to take the plunge and attempt the project. I figured it was worth the $35 risk for a unique model that would also fit in with the other

buildings in the city. The result, Union Station, is free-lanced yet looks realistic.

I found this project to be quite enjoyable. Nothing about it was difficult or tedious, and even a little experience with Magnuson kits will enable you to use these techniques.

GETTING STARTED

Although I used the front walls and doorway of the Magnuson no. 530 municipal building for my model, and that kit is no longer available, this technique will work with any of the Magnuson cast-resin kits. I removed the sidewalk notch from the bottom of each part and eliminated the decorative trim above the cornice.

I drew a curved line on my layout to follow the edge of the sidewalk, which in turn follows the line of the tracks. I then made a tracing of this plan on paper as shown in fig. 1 and took it to the kitchen, where the crucial phase of construction would take place.

I gathered the necessary utensils — a saucepan and an oven mitt — while my wife Lisa looked on curiously. Normally just mildly amused by my enthusiasm for the hobby, she really thought I'd gone off the deep end with this one, especially when I started boiling the walls. But more on that in a minute.

COOKING THE WALLS

I began by shaping the long wall section to the left of the doorway. First I filled the saucepan with water and heated it to a near boil. Then, facing the moment of truth, I submerged the left half of this piece into the hot water

as shown in fig. 2. After about 30 seconds, the piece had sufficiently softened, so I removed it from the water and began shaping it. Be sure to wear the oven mitt during this step as the piece will be quite hot.

Using the tracing as a template, I formed a gentle curve in the wall as shown in fig. 3. The ink from the marker I used for the tracing bled when I touched the piece to it. To prevent this, use a pencil instead of a marker.

I made some minor adjustments, removing the few small kinks that had developed. You'll need to work fairly quickly during this process. As the part cools it becomes more brittle, and after about a minute it will be impossible to make further corrections without starting over. The key is to get the water hot enough and leave the piece in long enough to be able to work it into its proper shape in one attempt.

A note of caution: If the water is too hot, the piece may warp badly. I suggest heating the water until you see surface bubbles form before immersing the piece. If it doesn't bend easily, you can raise the temperature of the water.

After I was satisfied with the shape, I formed the right side of this section using the same procedure. You may find, as I did, that small cracks develop on the face of the part during the curving process. This is due to the sharpness of the curve. If this happens, patch the cracks with spackling compound. When that part of the section has dried, sand it to match the other surface detail. I took the part to the layout to make sure the curve was correct, then set it aside.

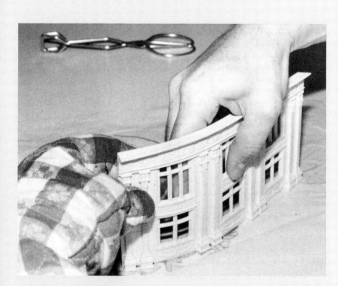

Fig. 3. SHAPING. Bend the wall to match the curve on the paper template. Try to get an even curve throughout the height of the wall.

Fig. 4. ADDING THE DOOR SECTION. After checking the curve of the short wall section, use epoxy to glue it to the short doorway.

Next comes the short wall to the right of the doorway. Because it's small, I heated the whole part at once, then bent it to the correct shape. I also brought this piece to the layout to check the accuracy of the curve, and then attached the doorway to its left side as shown in fig. 4. This was tricky as there wasn't much of an edge on either part for a flush fit. I filed both edges slightly so a secure joint could be made. Working directly on the layout, I bonded these two parts with five-minute epoxy.

I next placed the two completed sections side by side — the longer left side wall and shorter doorway and right side wall — and found that they were slightly misaligned. The overall curve was correct, but the long wall was slightly out of vertical, causing the misalignment. I corrected this problem by reheating the long wall and reshaping it, after which I test-fit the two parts together as shown in fig. 5. Then I filed the edges where these two sections would be joined, and when satisfied with the fit, prepared both parts for painting and weathering.

PAINTING

I began by airbrushing both sections with a base coat of Floquil 110085 Antique White. I followed with an overspray of sandstone color consisting of 65 percent Floquil 110073 Rust, 25 percent 110074 Boxcar Red, and 10 percent 110081 Earth. The idea was to have a little of the white show through to provide a coarse, grainy effect. In areas where I wasn't too heavy-handed with the airbrush this worked nicely.

I brush-painted the windows and door with Earth, then weathered everything with a wash of India ink diluted in alcohol. I followed this with streaks of powdered chalks here and there using gray, white, and brown pastels. These added interesting shadings to the basic color.

My one piece of advice on weathering with chalks is to go lightly at first and progressively add darker colors, stopping *before* you think you've done enough. I never seem to get this right and will often wash everything off and start over, just as I did on this model.

WINDOW GLAZING AND AWNINGS

I used some frosted acetate that I had on hand rather than the material supplied in the kit since the acetate was easy to shape. I built the awnings from styrene as shown in fig. 6. I spray-painted the awnings with Model Master 1913 Medium Green, weathered them with the India-ink wash and pastel chalks, and set them aside.

ASSEMBLY

Cementing the wall sections together was the first step of assembly. I did this on the layout to ensure an accurate match to the curve of the sidewalk. While the epoxy set, I stepped back and viewed the model from various locations to see whether everything looked correct. I reinforced the assembly by cementing scrap styrene on the back of the wall sections across the joints. I filled any visible joints with spackling compound, and painted and weathered it to blend with the rest of the model.

I fabricated the two hidden back walls from cardstock and stripwood, saving the walls supplied in the kit for future projects. I painted the visible part of these walls (the coping above the roof), then glued them in place to form the pie-wedge-shaped finished shell.

To make the roof I gingerly turned the model over and traced its inner outline on a piece of cardstock. I cut this piece using a sharp hobby knife, laminated it to a sheet of sandpaper, and trimmed it to an exact fit. After adding reinforcing stripwood underneath to prevent warping, I brush-painted the roof with Floquil 110013 Grimy Black. I cemented stripwood roof supports about 1/8" below the top of the cornice, then glued the roof in place. For added interest I cemented ventilation equipment and other details near the back of the model.

FRAME SIGN

I like signs. They add pizazz to structures and lend authenticity to the overall look. I made the frame sign using Plastruct channel stock and 3/4" menuboard letters purchased at a stationery supply store. I've used these types of letters on other models and really like them. They come in different sizes and styles and are relatively inexpensive. The only adjustment that may be required is reducing their thickness to improve the appearance. Figure 6 shows how I built the sign.

The last step was to cement the awnings in place. These added a nice finishing touch to the model.

I hope you'll be able to incorporate some of these ideas into a curved-front building for your layout. ◘

Fig. 5. JOINING THE WALLS. Test-fit the two main wall sections. When you're satisfied with the fit, use epoxy to glue them together.

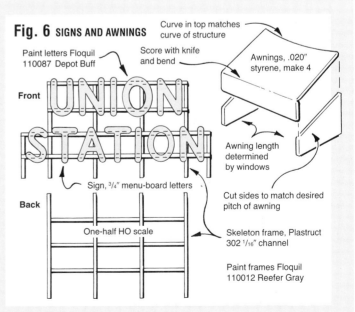

Fig. 6 SIGNS AND AWNINGS

Curve in top matches curve of structure

Paint letters Floquil 110087 Depot Buff

Score with knife and bend

Awnings, .020" styrene, make 4

Front

UNION STATION

Back

Sign, 3/4" menu-board letters

One-half HO scale

Awning length determined by windows

Cut sides to match desired pitch of awning

Skeleton frame, Plastruct 302 1/16" channel

Paint frames Floquil 110012 Reefer Gray

Fig. 1. The author says that it's not just the building under demolition but the complete scene that makes it an attention-getter for a model city.

Building demolition

Build it up so it looks like it's coming down

BY EARL SMALLSHAW
PHOTOS BY THE AUTHOR

Fig. 2. Earl doesn't like to waste effort on parts of a model that won't be seen. This side of the burned-out building faces the backdrop, so the side wall to the left has no exterior detail and the end wall isn't modeled at all!

WHAT GOES UP must come down. That old, old saying probably started when air travel was in its infancy! When you think about it, it applies to buildings, too, whether the cause is wind, flood, earthquake, fire, or "redevelopment."

The Connecticut Fire Extinguisher Co. building came to grief, embarrassingly enough, by fire. A clogged flue caused a potbellied stove on the third floor to overheat, and the heat ignited a drum of solvent stored closer to the stove than it should have been. The fire quickly spread to the wood-shingled roof. By the time the fire was put out, half the roof was destroyed and part of the third floor had collapsed onto the floor below. The building was too far gone to save, so the wrecking crew was called.

That sets the stage. For some time I've wanted to model a building being demolished. It's a test of creativity and imagination and adds interest to a city scene. I won't give step-by-step instructions. If I can help you understand how to make sagging floors, a burned-out roof, and other features, I hope you'll have your own ideas for a building demolition scene. My scene is for an HO railroad, but the methods I'll tell you about can be used for any scale.

Keep in mind that to be convincing your scene must be logical. Think through where the fire started and how it spread. Consider what a floor would look like once part of its support had burned away. A big part of the challenge is to visualize and build a structure with its interior partially exposed.

BASIC BUILDING

Since I was building a background structure, I "cheaped out" by using parts from my scrap box rather than trashing a new kit. I started with a leftover wall from a Magnuson bank; because I didn't have any matching parts, I made the remaining walls of illustration board. In fig. 1, the Magnuson wall is on the left.

The end wall is made of two layers of illustration board to match the thickness of the Magnuson wall. While I scribed horizontal mortar lines on the new wall to give it texture, I didn't worry about making them uniform. The windows were cut to match the size and location of the

Magnuson's, and I added frames and sills made from stripwood and styrene.

On the first floor I cut a shipping/receiving door, glued a roughly textured beam along its bottom edge, and added two Grandt Line nut-bolt-washer castings to "hold" this sill in place. The office entrance with its stairs and railing is styrene, and the small peaked roof is cardstock.

Using my band saw I cut the Magnuson wall and the new end to look partially demolished. It's up to you to decide just how much to leave standing, but after rough shaping make short horizontal and vertical cuts along the brick courses. You cant a stepped contour since brick walls tend to separate at the mortar joints.

I painted the wall exteriors with Floquil Earth and used a brick-red color along the edges exposed by demolition. The Magnuson wall had to be painted at this point because I

wanted to paint a sign directly on it, and it's much easier to apply lettering before assembly.

The first floor was cut from illustration board. Instead of using expensive stripwood where it would hardly be seen, I drew wood floorboards with pan and ink on IBM-card stock. Watercolors let me paint the boards without covering the ink—brown hues mixed with a little black are best. I glued the cardstock flooring to the illustration board, reinforced the floor with ¼"-square balsa to bring it up to a loading door's level, then assembled the side and end walls with the floor.

My philosophy is to model only the parts of a building that will be seen on the layout, so the far wall is plain illustration board detailed on the inside alone. I didn't even bother to make a second end. The far corner of my model is cut off to fit against the backdrop, so the missing wall would not have been visible. See fig. 2.

The window openings in the back wall were cut to match those of the Magnuson. Although I installed the window frames and acetate glazing at this time, I didn't cement the back wall the the building yet. It's helpful to have the wall for checking the alignment of the upper floors, but I needed to add interior details, and that's easier before the back wall is installed.

I didn't add any interior details on the first floor for the simple reason that not much would be visible in the completed model. However, I did cut several blocks of balsa and painted them with Floquil Earth to represent cartons on the shipping and receiving dock. I also scattered a few loose boards—strips of cardstock—on the first floor. Then I dusted this level liberally with black chalk dust.

UPPER FLOORS

The second floor sustained some damage when the fire burned through the floor above. In addition, the front corner of the second floor was already exposed by demolition. Consequently, I had to model at least part of the floor system in some detail, as is shown in fig. 3. As with the first story, the basic floor is illustration board with cardstock flooring.

Fig. 3. This closeup shows how part of the second floor's structure appears to have been exposed by demolition. Earl included the lavatory to add interest up front while concealing undetailed areas behind.

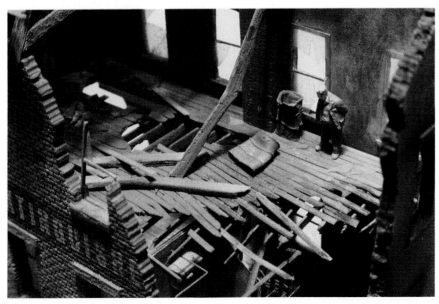

Fig. 4. On the third floor the fire burned through much of the floor and left heavy deposits of soot and debris. It's not a good place to be walking around, especially with the wrecker's ball poised outside!

Fig. 5. The fire didn't leave much of the roof, and what remains is going fast. Earl used individual Campbell shingles and stripwood stringers to model the exposed structure around the roof's burned edges. He charred the stringers and trusses with a torch for extra authenticity.

I let the exposed corner of this flooring hand over the illustration board and cut along the inked lines to separate the ends of individual boards. Some hang down, broken, while others are just missing.

Using stripwood, I added scale 2 x 8 floor joists under the overhanging flooring. The joists, too, were cut jagged, broken ends and allowed to sag a little.

Wanting to block off the second floor to limit visibility. I recalled an SS Limited kit for an old-fashioned toilet (no longer available) that I'd acquired some time ago. I don't use interior detail in many structures, but here the interior is part of the exterior, so the toilet could be used to add some visible character.

The toilet became the main feature of a severely damaged lavatory, behind a foreground wall of which just a skeleton of studding remains. I built this out of scale 2 x 4 stripwood and even included a few lath strips made from thin strips of paper. The remaining walls are cardstock.

A common wall treatment in years past was waist-high paneling, often made with vertical planks of decorative wood, called "wainscotting." I drew this in with pen and ink, then colored the wainscotting brown and the upper walls yellow. A few barrels, broken boards, and pieces of glass (acetate) completed this floor. Like the first, it got a generous application of "soot" in the form of black chalk dust.

Some details on this floor because directly from my prototype demolition photos. An example is the remaining lavatory plumbing. One pipe is still in place despite the demolition, while another hangs twisted in space, presumably snagged by falling debris. I doubt that I'd have thought to include these pipes if I hadn't noticed them in photographs.

A second detail taken from my photos is the piece of ceiling hanging below the second floor. Not only does this seem realistic, he also helps block views of the rest of the first floor. Finally, there is the second floor window frame that is broken but hasn't yet fallen. Delicately balanced, you know it's about to drop with the next blow from the wrecker's ball.

The top floor, shown in fig. 4, was the most challenging. Again, I started with illustration board and cardstock. For places where the floor had burned through, I cut away the illustration board, then cut the cardstock that bridges these gaps into individual boards. I wanted to make the floor sag as though it had lost most of its support. Some joists are suspended in space from the floorboards. Though I also cut a stairwell into this floor, I didn't build a staircase because it wouldn't be seen.

Once the top floor was in place, I installed the back wall and added the chimney, which has survived the fire to stand like a sentry over the building's remains. The chimney is balsa scribed to represent brick. It's painted to match the interior walls at its lower end, while above the roof line it's brick red. Be sure to continue the chimney through the lower floors if it can be seen. I also built a partition, with a door drawn on it, at the back of the third floor to help hide the absence of the fourth wall.

To complete the top floor I scattered

Fig. 6. Rubble is inevitable with demolition, and Earl explains how to make convincing piles of the stuff. Color is part of this, and back in fig. 1 you can see how Earl's rubble matches the colors of his building.

some boards, glass, and collapsed drums (by Alloy Forms) here and there. The fire started here, and the damaged drums indicate an explosion and heat. This level was also filled with soot, and I made the interior walls extra black by using an artist's stub—a small stick of rolled paper—to rub the chalk into intense streaks.

ROOF

I made several large balsa trusses to support the roof, assembling then in a jig so they'd be uniform. I painted them dark brown and glued them to the front and back walls about 6 scale feet apart. As you can see in fig. 5, the foreground truss has been dislodged and hangs precariously, adding a little suspense.

For the subroof I used thin cardboard from the back of a notepad, cut to a contour depicting a badly damaged, burned out roof. Where the cardboard ended I glued stripwood stringers to the trusses. Distress the ends of these boards and remove others where the edges of the roof are exposed. Over the subroof I applied Campbell shingles in short strips. Where the roof was burned out, I cut a few individual shingles from the strips and glued them to the remaining stringers.

Now for some excitement! Using s small propane soldering torch with a needle-thin flame, I carefully burned the edges of the exposed stringers. My aim was to char the edges of these boards without letting them catch fire. When that did happen, I quickly pulled the torch away and blew out the flames. I didn't use water for fear of destroying the thin wood and cardstock structural details and of leaving grossly out-of-scale water spots.

I burned the trusses, too, and they gave me the most trouble. Once they started to char, the wood continued to burn like a wick. Only through constant blowing was I able to keep them from burning up, though they did end up nicely charred.

DRESSING THE SCENE

For a final "sooting" of the whole building I applied Grimy Black paint with an airbrush. The window openings closest to the fire were heavily blackened where smoke would have billowed out. I also touched up the interior walls with the airbrush where the smoke would have been most prevalent. A light overall haze of Grimy Black on the outside walls took away any clean look.

Using a fine pen, I drew cracks in the wall where the wrecker's ball was hit but not yet broken through. I applied brown and black chalk dust with the artist's stub to emphasize the "hit."

No demolition scene is complete without piles of rubble and debris like those in fig. 6. These fall into two categories: brick, mortar, wood, and other nondescript types of mostly disposable material; and identifiable and salvageable material, such as girders, pipes, and oil drums.

To be convincing your rubble piles must have sufficient mass. Laying rubble about as you might sow grass seed is just too one-dimensional for creditability. I built mounds of plaster around the building to create large masses of debris. As the plaster dried, I buried larger details in it, like wooden beams, girders, and other heavy things that would look out of place just laying on top.

Once the plaster dries, paint everything except the buried details dull black. That way no white spots will show in the completed pile. Beginning at the base of the pile, start adding building debris that represents the type and color of the structure itself. If the brick wall, for example, is painted green, then much of the brick rubble would be similarly colored. Except for broken edges, pieces of wood flooring would match that of the structure's remaining floor. Those edges would be raw, newly exposed wood. Just use common sense when selecting and coloring your rubble.

In fig. 1, part of the property-line fence has been knocked down by the crane as it maneuvered to attack what's left of the fire extinguisher building. Two women from the adjacent tenement building are in a highly vocal discussion about just who will pay for all this!

Six buildings from three

Techniques for making your Magnuson buildings go farther

BY EARL SMALLSHAW
PHOTOS BY THE AUTHOR

COMMERCIAL structure kits generally come with four walls: front, back, and two sides. Assembled as the manufacturer suggests, the structure you end up with will be a nice-looking, four-sided one. But, when you place it on the layout can you see all four sides? Do you need the back wall? Or could you do without the back and one side? Could you substitute a blank wall of illustration board and use the replaced wall in another structure? There is no purpose in modeling something that will never be seen.

I'm currently building Middletown on the Middletown & Mystic Mines RR. It will be comprised of many city structures, all placed closely together, compressed into a 9″ x 40″ area. In anticipation of this project I had acquired some Magnuson kits (Victoria Falls Hotel, Grain Exchange, and Bank of Victoria Falls among them), but with limited space available, I couldn't build the structures without modifications. Happily, these changes also allowed me to stretch my modeling dollars.

Since Middletown can be viewed only from the front and one side, I wouldn't be needing all of the walls of each structure. In fact, I couldn't fit them in if I wanted to! It quickly became apparent that, with a little work, these extra walls could serve as the basis for other structures — totally unlike the originals.

My first structure was to be the Middletown movie theater (fig. 1). I had to place this one in the foreground so that the lighted marquee and chase lights could be easily seen. (If you knew how much effort went into the marquee, you would understand why.)

The basis for the theater was the Grain Exchange building. There was room for only two walls (front and side), forming an oblique angle to conform to the space available — a triangular area, bisected by the yard approach track. The roof, visible from above in its entirety,

Fig. 1. The Middletown Theater's two walls were originally the front and a side wall from Magnuson's Grain Exchange. An animated marquee and fire escape add character to the front and side, and an SS Limited billboard, carrying an ad from an old MR, adds interest to the roof.

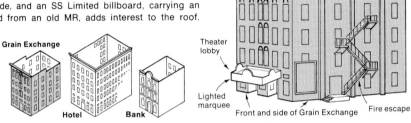

Fig. 2. Using one side of Magnuson's Victoria Falls Hotel and the back wall of their Grain Exchange, the author built Small & Shaw Mfg. The only changes he made were the addition of the loading door for freight cars, the roof over the addition, and the elevator structure on the roof.

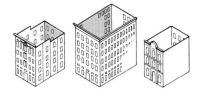

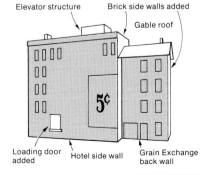

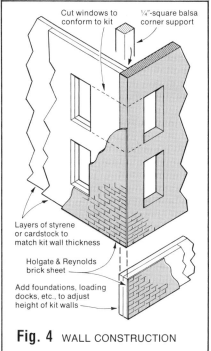

Fig. 3. Poli Ice Co. was made from the back wall of the hotel and half of a side wall from the Grain Exchange. The other walls are illustration board covered with Holgate & Reynolds brick. The freight platform and roof, and the icing platform were made from basswood and cardstock.

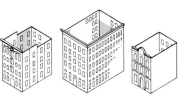

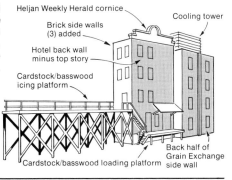

Heljan Weekly Herald cornice
Brick side walls (3) added
Hotel back wall minus top story
Cardstock/basswood icing platform
Cooling tower
Back half of Grain Exchange side wall
Cardstock/basswood loading platform

Cut windows to conform to kit
¼"-square balsa corner support
Layers of styrene or cardstock to match kit wall thickness
Holgate & Reynolds brick sheet
Add foundations, loading docks, etc., to adjust height of kit walls

Fig. 4 WALL CONSTRUCTION

had to be modeled in a trapezoidal shape to imply that all walls were in place. In fact, one of the back corners of the roof overhangs the track, although this is not apparent to the viewer.

From this beginning, I now had one side and the back of the Grain Exchange left over. Each of these walls became part of two other structures.

First, I combined a side wall from the Victoria Falls Hotel with the leftover back wall of the Grain Exchange to come up with Small & Shaw Mfg. See fig. 2. The back wall of the hotel and the other side of the Grain Exchange, modified as in fig. 3, resulted in the Poli Ice Co.

In each case I combined the kit walls with illustration-board walls covered with Holgate & Reynolds brick sheet. See fig. 4. I used ¼" balsa strips in the corners for support and added windows, modified to conform to the kit's windows, as required.

The city block on a hillside, shown under construction in fig. 5, consists of the front and back walls of the Bank of Victoria Falls, and the leftover front and side of the hotel. I left the front of the bank pretty much as it comes from the kit, adding only an abbreviated side, built as shown in fig. 4. I modified the back wall of the bank to represent a small shop by cutting in a show window and adding corbels along the roof edge. The remaining two hotel walls make up the rest of the city block.

I started out with three Magnuson buildings and ended up with what at least appear to be six buildings. Modify the kits as I have, or do it your own way. You're limited only by your imagination. ✿

Fig. 5. The author built this city block from (left to right) the front of the Bank of Victoria Falls, its back (modified), and the front and side of the Victoria Falls Hotel. Note that these structures, when installed on the layout, will be on a hillside. The bases had to be modified accordingly.

Front wall of bank
Back wall of bank with added trim
Front and side of hotel
Brick side wall added
Original window enlarged to shop window
Foundations added to match street slope

This scene on Dave Bascom's HO scale Ontario & Eastern layout shows that it's possible to build a realistic urban scene in a small area.

The other side of town

Modeling an effective urban scene in a small area

BY EARL SMALLSHAW
PHOTOS BY THE AUTHOR

THERE'S AN unspoken rule within the Hartford Workshop, an informal group of modelers in central Connecticut, that all final scenery work be left to each individual member. However, now that our respective layouts are nearing completion (if any layout is ever considered complete), I've found my meeting nights confined to "finish" work, while wiring and other tasks are given to other, much more qualified members of the group.

I don't mind, since this way I get to experiment with new techniques on someone else's layout. When I'm assigned a challenging scenery task, I always answer, "Sure, what do I care? It's not *my* layout." They never take me seriously.

The urban scene I built on Dave Bascom's HO scale Ontario & Eastern RR is one example. I started by making some sketches of a small urban scene for a 22″ x 30″ area adjacent to a bridge complex that Dave was building. This scene could include both kit and scratchbuilt structures, I told Dave. He pulled out three shopping bags full of Design Preservation Models and Magnuson kits he had collected, essentially saying "Put up or shut up!" The results, shown in the lead photo, indicate that an effective city scene can be built in a small space.

STREET

Figure 1 shows the overall layout of the scene. The track and bridge abutments were already in place, and Dave had sketched in the street and sidewalks, so that's where I started. The street simulates a cobblestone surface that's been paved over with blacktop. I

cut small sections of Brawa no. 2805 cobblestone into circles and ellipses, then glued them in random fashion to the street base.

Then I added a thin mixture of plaster of paris, applying it with a wide spatula to make the street surface as smooth as possible. When I had finished, the plaster was just thick enough to blend with the top surface of the cobblestone. I finished the street as shown in fig. 2.

I made the sidewalks the same way, using cardboard forms to establish the curb. I applied a thin plaster mix and blended it with the surrounding areas. Once the plaster had dried, I scribed expansion joints into the sidewalk with a hobby knife. The curb crumbled in one area so I applied glue to hold the pieces just as they crumbled. In a neighborhood like this, curbs and sidewalks are often in disrepair.

The street level is lower where it dips under the bridge, leaving the sidewalk higher than normal. I installed a Central Valley railing on both sides of the street to keep cars and pedestrians apart where the sidewalk narrows.

STRUCTURES

I scratchbuilt and kitbashed the structures to fit this situation. There are many other structures available that will work just as well as those I used.

Both Bascom & Sons Manufacturing and B&S Warehouse No. 1 are scratchbuilt as shown in fig. 3. Exact dimensions aren't included, as you can easily adjust the sizes of these buildings to suit the needs of your layout. There are only two walls to the manufacturing building and three to the warehouse. I don't model anything that can't be seen.

I painted the styrene structure brick red, a mixture of Floquil 110074 Boxcar Red, 110020 Caboose Red, 110030 Reefer Orange, and 110013 Grimy Black. I've never measured exact proportions — I just mix the colors until they look right. The windows are Floquil 110011 Reefer White. I used white and black chalk dust to age all the structures.

To overcome the vacant look of the styrene building, I made several cardboard "profiles," simple rectangular shapes to simulate machinery and boxes. I colored these using splashes of red, brown, and yellow. Tabs at each end of the profiles were glued to the walls, with the profiles about 1/2" behind the windows at each floor level.

I lettered all the structures with various styles of dry-transfer lettering. I use C-Thru brand; several brands and styles can be found in art supply stores and some hobby shops.

BACKDROP

I used a portion of an Instant Horizons freight yard backdrop, trimmed along its bottom edge to place the street level of the backdrop in line with the foreground street. As fig. 4 shows, the result is amazing! When looking down the street at eye level, it appears as if the truck on the backdrop is just over a slight rise in the street. I airbrushed the backdrop with a light coat of Floquil 110086 Grime to tone down the colors.

The Bascom Mfg. building, shown in the lead photo, was made using DPM's Modular Wall System. To build the structure as shown, you'll need one pack each of wall sections 301-01, 301-02, 301-11, and 301-14; and two packs of 301-08. These modules make it easy to design a structure to fit your own space requirements with very credible results.

I modified the structure by cutting one of the freight doors down the middle and

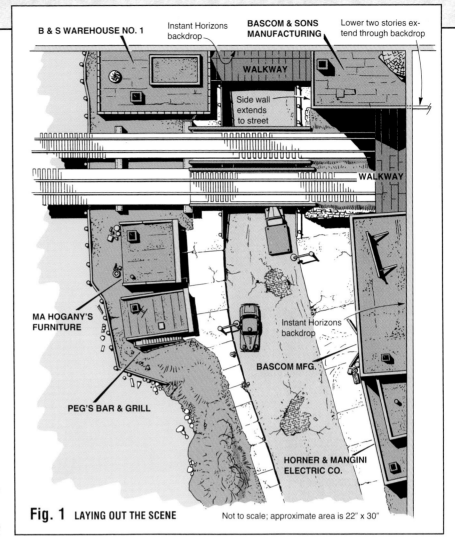

Fig. 1 LAYING OUT THE SCENE Not to scale; approximate area is 22″ x 30″

gluing each half open. I added bits of styrene in the shape of strap hinges and made wire handles from .010″ brass wire. Inside, I made a receiving platform with boxes, crates, and barrels. For the roof I scratchbuilt a billboard using stripwood and a Conoco sign from the September 1975 issue of MODEL RAILROADER.

The whole structure received a coat of my brick red formula, and the windows and doors were painted with Floquil 110081 Earth. The sign lettering is 36-point Eurostyle bold. I distressed

the lettering by lightly sanding it with fine sandpaper.

The end wall looked a little bare, so I added a Coca-Cola sign to it. From signs I made for my own layout, I created a stencil of the "Coca-Cola" — I describe the technique in *Scenery Tips and Techniques from Model Railroader Magazine* (Kalmbach Publishing Co.). I painted a red panel on the wall, outlined it with a white border, and used an airbrush to apply the "Coca-Cola." The remaining words are dry transfers.

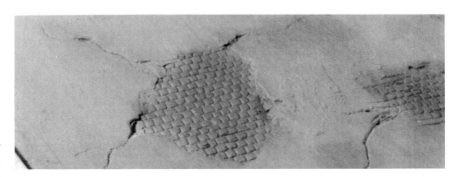

Fig. 2. COBBLESTONE STREET. After the plaster had dried, the author cleaned it from the cobblestone surface. He followed that by adding cracks and small holes with a hobby knife. Then he used fine sandpaper to smooth out unprototypical bits of plaster on the street surface.

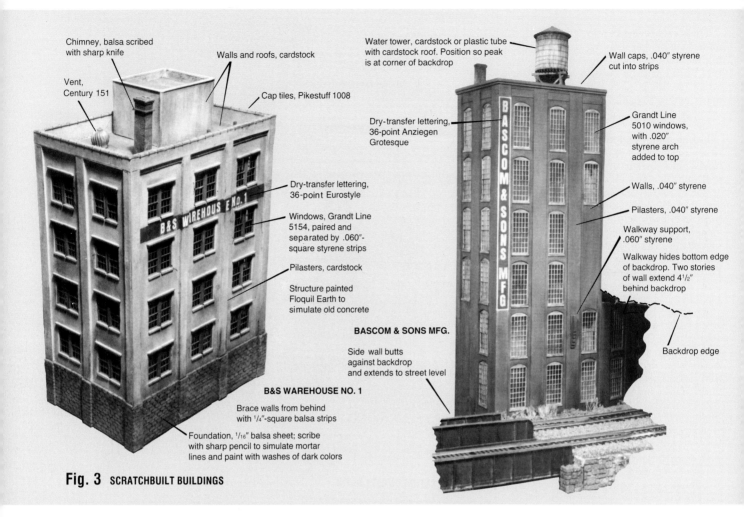

Chimney, balsa scribed with sharp knife

Vent, Century 151

Walls and roofs, cardstock

Cap tiles, Pikestuff 1008

Dry-transfer lettering, 36-point Eurostyle

Windows, Grandt Line 5154, paired and separated by .060"-square styrene strips

Pilasters, cardstock

Structure painted Floquil Earth to simulate old concrete

B&S WAREHOUSE NO. 1

Brace walls from behind with 1/4"-square balsa strips

Foundation, 1/16" balsa sheet; scribe with sharp pencil to simulate mortar lines and paint with washes of dark colors

Water tower, cardstock or plastic tube with cardstock roof. Position so peak is at corner of backdrop

Dry-transfer lettering, 36-point Anziegen Grotesque

Wall caps, .040" styrene cut into strips

Grandt Line 5010 windows, with .020" styrene arch added to top

Walls, .040" styrene

Pilasters, .040" styrene

Walkway support, .060" styrene

Walkway hides bottom edge of backdrop. Two stories of wall extend 4 1/2" behind backdrop

Backdrop edge

BASCOM & SONS MFG.

Side wall butts against backdrop and extends to street level

Fig. 3 SCRATCHBUILT BUILDINGS

STORES

Horner & Mangini Electric, shown in the lead photo, was a kitbash of DPM's no. 104 B. Moore Catalog Showroom. I used parts of the rear and side walls to make the fourth and fifth stories. Harold Horner and Paul Mangini spent several nights freeing the layout from electrical gremlins, so it seemed only fitting that a structure be named for them for their effort.

The lettering on the windows was done with dry transfers applied directly to acetate. I overlaid this acetate with another piece to prevent the lettering from being scratched off. Apply this overlay with Scotch tape along the edges. Don't do as I first did by using styrene cement to bond the two pieces. The cement attacked the lettering through capillary action.

I airbrushed this structure with Floquil 110009 Primer and painted the windows and doors with Floquil 110048 Coach Green. The roof is 1/16" posterboard. I sprayed it with contact cement, then applied fine sand to simulate a gravel roof. A balsa chimney and Century ventilator completed the roof details.

Across the street is Peg's Bar & Grill, named for Dave's wife. It's a DPM no. 105 Skip's Chicken & Ribs kit with an outside staircase added. I made the upper window into a paneled door, fabricated from pieces of .010" styrene. Then I built a platform from scribed styrene with 2 x 6 styrene strips for support and added Central Valley stairs and a railing made from styrene strips.

The circus poster is a Finescale Miniatures sign. I prepare my paper signs by lightly sanding the back until the sandpaper just about comes through the front. When applied with thinned white glue, the sign nestles right onto the surface on which it's applied. I also curled up a couple of corners to simulate age.

I painted the large sign directly on the wall, starting with a black panel outlined in white. I painted the "Peg's" freehand and added white shadow lines. I also painted a beer mug (including beer and foam). The "Bar & Grill" are dry transfers. The front sign is simply a strip of styrene painted black with dry-transfer lettering applied.

To hide the lack of interior detail, I clouded the windows by spraying Krylon

Matte (any clear dull finish will work) from the *inside* of the structure. One or two thin coats is enough to distort any images inside.

I finished by adding a TV aerial to the roof. I made it from .010" brass wire, with a couple of shim brass straps to secure it to the chimney.

The "Ma Hogany Furniture" store next door is a Magnuson Gemini Building. I added a sign in the same fashion as the bar and placed large signs in the windows advertising furniture sales.

WALKWAYS

Next, I built the two walkways as shown in fig. 5. I made supports for both of them using .060" styrene strips, glued together in a stepped fashion, with all strips trimmed flush at the top as shown in fig. 3. I painted each support to match the structures and then installed them.

FINAL DETAILS

I applied white glue to the ground under the bridge and sprinkled plaster chips on the surface, creating an arid rubble effect. I painted this with various browns and grays, typical of an

Fig. 4. BACKDROP. Cutting the bottom of the backdrop to match the street creates a very realistic scene. The walkway and bridge hide the fact that the buildings are against the backdrop.

area such as this. Vegetation was limited to weeds here and there, with just a touch of Woodland Scenics turf. Scraps of wood, old tires, and other assorted junk were also added.

I made a bulkhead along the water's edge using 1/16" balsa. I scribed the boards with a sharp pencil, painted the strip with Primer, then applied a thin wash of black paint to darken the cracks and age the wood. Posts are 1/8" wood dowel, drawn across a rough file to add grain, then painted and weathered like

the wall. The height of each post varies slightly, and the tops are cut at an angle.

I used plaster for the water, textured to simulate choppy waves, and painted the surface with artist's oil colors using black, deep blue, green, and a touch of yellow. Dave applied several coats of gloss wood finish for the water surface.

The Mountain States Ford squad car pokes a little fun at Paul Mangini, a police officer. We removed a door from the kit body, fashioned a new door from styrene, and glued it open. I'm not sure

whether the rushing policemen are raiding the upstairs apartment or just making a "visit."

Other figures ("Dave," near the office door), sea gulls, animals, and vehicles give life to the scene.

This scene wasn't difficult to create. Similar space should be available on all but the smallest of layouts. I hope I've inspired you to try urban modeling by creating a scene for your railroad. With all the city and industrial structures now available, it's easier than ever. ⚙

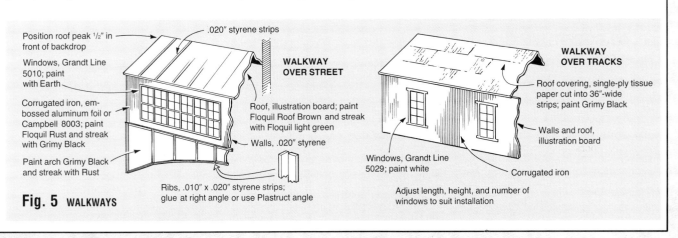

Position roof peak 1/2" in front of backdrop

.020" styrene strips

WALKWAY OVER STREET

Windows, Grandt Line 5010; paint with Earth

Corrugated iron, embossed aluminum foil or Campbell 8003; paint Floquil Rust and streak with Grimy Black

Roof, illustration board; paint Floquil Roof Brown and streak with Floquil light green

Walls, .020" styrene

Paint arch Grimy Black and streak with Rust

Ribs, .010" x .020" styrene strips; glue at right angle or use Plastruct angle

Fig. 5 WALKWAYS

WALKWAY OVER TRACKS

Roof covering, single-ply tissue paper cut into 36"-wide strips; paint Grimy Black

Walls and roof, illustration board

Corrugated iron

Windows, Grandt Line 5029; paint white

Adjust length, height, and number of windows to suit installation

Above. At Industrial and Mill streets in Los Angeles a real diesel switcher creeps through the curved brick wall canyon. Warning signs at the entrances indicate "Not sufficient clearance for man on side of car," and they're not kidding. Note the bricked-up windows on the left side.

Left. An Athearn SW1500 lettered for the Southern Pacific squirms through close clearances at the Phillips Poultry Co. The spur into the Los Angeles Soap Co. at the backdrop is too shallow to receive a car. The yellow board gates, along with the overpass, help to disguise the opening.

Curved tracks and close quarters

A compact arrangement for two industries served by a single spur

BY ROBERT SMAUS
PHOTOS BY THE AUTHOR

THE SMALL size of my HO layout (3'-0" x 10'-6") encouraged me to concentrate my modeling on railroading in congested industrial areas. Among some aging tracks on the west side of the Los Angeles River, I found an unusual track arrangement and two especially interesting structures that would make good-looking models. One of the benefits of the arrangement shown here is the way it disguises a spur track that runs off the edge of my layout.

The real tracks no longer see the traffic they once did. As far back as November 1952 only one tiger-striped Southern Pacific switcher was required to pull the few freight cars up the embankment and into the industrial area awaiting redevelopment. Most of the businesses have moved to the suburbs, though the Phillips Poultry Co., housed in a most unusual building, still receives an occasional mix of agricultural equipment, and the Los Angeles Soap Co., in business since the 1860s, ships an occasional load of White King laundry detergent back East.

Around the turn of the century when this part of town was the commercial heart of Los Angeles, space was at a premium. This accounts for the unusual shape of the poultry supplier's warehouse, shaped like a wedge of cheese with the rails curving as they make their way through a thicket of buildings. On the way to the poultry and soap complexes, the curved spur track (Santa Fe property) crosses old Pacific Electric tracks, now owned by the SP. A small two-tone gray tower, which has not been in use for many years, still guards the crossing.

THE MODELS

The two commercial buildings were my first models. On the real Phillips Poultry structure the shortest wall is more than 100 feet long, but the curving rails seem to make as tight a turn as they do on my foreshortened model with its 11" radius. The clearances are definitely tight on the curve. I cut up the walls from two Life-Like Belvedere Downtown Hotel kits, rearranged them, and glued them to a ½" plywood base. The curved walls I cut from Holgate & Reynolds O scale brick sheet material (matches the Life-Like bricks).

The cornice, augmented with styrene strip, came from a Model Die Casting Great American Buildings kit. I used Grandt Line nut-bolt-washer castings for the wall reinforcing (absolutely necessary in earthquake-prone L. A.). My beginner's mistakes are hidden to my satisfaction with spackling paste used as grout at the wall joints.

Carefully positioned rusting pipes and conduits further disguise the wall joints, and an awesome gap between the first two floors is hidden beneath a building-wide sign made with dry transfer lettering. By the time I had built the smaller of the two sections, I had discovered pastel chalks and was able to effectively weather the signs and bricks.

The Los Angeles Soap Co. is a low-profile kitbash of two Model Power Burlington Mills factory kits. I did a better job of joining the wall sections, and I didn't need to grout the joints. I simply painted the brick with Floquil Boxcar Red paint.

I tried to capture the flavor of the building without getting too literal, since it is smothered with details. The feature I like most is the elevated walkway between the two building halves since it helps hide the track that runs off the edge of the layout. I made this feature with Campbell corrugated siding, Plastruct angle, and Grandt Line windows. Almost every other detail came from the Model Power kits, bonanzas of miscellaneous parts.

The dirt I used for ground cover is real and taken from downtown Los Angeles. Using matte medium as a fixative for the scenic materials, I set the scene in early winter. In L. A. this means a mix

There's a small working yard in the foreground of Robert Smaus's HO scale layout, where the truss bridge (upper left) passes over tracks in a depressed area behind the poultry building. Small details like the switch stands, fences, warning signs, and handcar setouts put the finishing touches on the scene.

of withered weeds from summer and new weeds coming to life with the first rains. Even with the help of friend Barry Swackhamer, it took several months to scenic and detail a 2-foot-square area.

These closely spaced structures with interwoven tracks are typical of what I want to accomplish on my layout. Watching a model switcher back in and out of this miniature complex, disappearing then reappearing, is just as fascinating as watching a real train work. ☼

Aging plastic cars

Using a small light bulb to soften the plastic

BY LOU SASSI
PHOTOS BY THE AUTHOR

ONE EVENING, while visiting a fellow model railroader's layout, I found myself admiring two of his gondolas. What made them stand out was that they looked used — well used, as a matter of fact. So, I asked my friend to tell me how he aged the cars. He told me Jim Coons had given him the cars.

Jim was present that evening, so I asked him how he had created the aged effect. First of all, he told me the cars were Athearn 50-foot gons (no. 1647) that he'd modified following Bill Mis-

chler's June 1985 Paint Shop feature, "Erie mill gon." His aging technique involved heating the cars with a soldering gun and creating bends and dents by flexing the hot plastic. I told Jim I was so impressed with the results he'd obtained that I was going to give his method a try.

I purchased several Athearn cars the next day and began experimenting. I found that the soldering gun was a little too touchy for me to control, so I started searching for other ways to heat the cars. What I found worked the best for me was a small 120-volt, 4-watt bulb placed against the plastic. This is the size bulb used in night lights. You can buy a candelabra socket and electrical

cord and make a little "work light." An easier way to do this would be to use a night light (with the reflector removed) plugged into an extension cord.

You can lay this small bulb right against the area of the car you wish to bend or dent and then just wait for the plastic to soften. See fig. 1. It takes only a minute or two. You can create dents, bends, and bulges by gently applying pressure to the model with either the hot bulb itself, or by using the side of a ball-point pen or pencil.

Since that first trial I've used this technique on a number of gondolas and hopper cars with excellent results. I further aged gondolas 9608 and 9635, shown in the photo above, by doing some carving with an X-acto knife. Then I repainted them. Repainting is not necessary. The two hopper cars shown in fig. 2 were aged using the same techniques, but they were not repainted.

I've found this aging method to be an easy way to add character to my rolling stock. I hope you do too. ♂

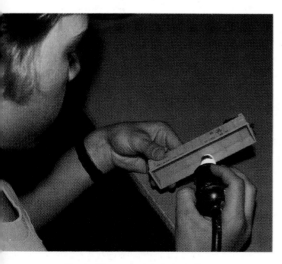

Fig. 1. Above. A night-light bulb in an extension cord socket held against the side of a car softens it in a minute or two allowing dents to be formed.
Fig. 2. Right. These hoppers were "beat up" in the same manner. No repainting is necessary.

HO scale Boston & Maine RS-3 no. 1542 hauls empty (more-or-less) scrap metal gons across Collins Creek on the return trip to Postabe from Adams.

Real scrap loads for your gons

The material is as near to you as your car

BY LOU SASSI

ONE FEBRUARY afternoon, while standing amidst the hills and dales surrounding my HO scale Postabe RR., I noticed something. There in the rail yards below me was an abundance of gondolas and hoppers all sharing the same feature: emptiness. Right, no lading of any type and no indication that there ever was one. What these cars needed was some loads or remnants of loads to give the impression that they really were in service.

Scale coal and gravel would suit the bill for the hoppers, especially since their destinations were the outlets for Buesing Coal Co. But what else could be used to create the effect of lading? A trip to the grocery store one chilly Northeastern morn unexpectedly gave me the answer.

Upon returning home from said trip I slammed shut the door of my 1970 Pontiac LeMans, and what to my surprise fell out of the rear wheel well? Scrap metal! Yes, real rusted, dirty, salty scrap metal. I immediately dropped my bag of groceries and ran to the house to fetch a paper cup. I scraped up a cupful of the muddy mess I had just discovered and brought it to the sink.

Using a kitchen sieve (this one happened to be railroad property used for grading sand) I washed away the mud and salt, and there before me was an accumulation of rusted scrap metal particles of various sizes. I dumped these remnants on an old newspaper to dry and then picked out and discarded what I considered oversize for my purpose.

Once satisfied with the texture of the remaining material, I located some suitable victims among my freight car roster and spread the particles along their floors. (My intent was to simulate the remains of a previous load, but a full load could be created by adding a false bottom and spreading a heavier mixture over it.)

Next I eye-dropped some wet water (water with one or two drops of household detergent added) onto the material. Then, with the same eye-dropper, I added a few drops of 2 parts water to 1 part white glue. Once this had dried, I lightly dry brushed some artist's ground pigments over the load. The photo shows the results.

Now, is there anyone out there interested in a lifetime supply of HO scrap metal disguised as a rusty old 1970 LeMans? ✿

The author's son, Adam Sassi, prospects for more scale scrap metal load material cleverly concealed beneath the paint of a 1970 Pontiac Lemans.

Urban scenery

How to build a city scene in any scale

BY EARL SMALLSHAW
PHOTOS BY THE AUTHOR

OF ALL model railroad scenery, an urban scene will draw the most attention from visitors. With the buildings, vehicles, people, signs, lights, and other details of a city, even the most spectacular mountain scenery can't compete.

An outstanding example of urban scenery is George Sellios' Franklin & South Manchester RR in the April 1987 issue of MODEL RAILROADER. I'll bet there wasn't a single reader who could turn past those photos without

a good, long look at each detailed scene. While we all don't have George's time, space, and resources, an urban scene of reasonable size can be achieved by almost any model railroader.

"But I have barely enough room for the track, much less for a small city," most modelers will say. Few of us have unlimited space, but there are many ways of "expanding" the space we do have with selective compression, mirrors, and the use of "air rights."

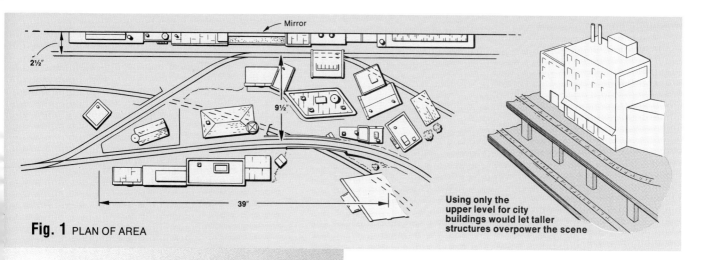

Mirror

2½"

9½"

39"

Fig. 1 PLAN OF AREA

Using only the
upper level for city
buildings would let taller
structures overpower the scene

Urban scenery, dramatic and interesting in itself, provides a justification for the railroad yards and terminals we like to model. Earl Smallshaw's city of Middletown is an urban scene built in a small space shared with track on two levels. Earl placed buildings on both the lower and upper levels to hide some of the track and help blend the city with the railroad.

MIDDLETOWN

I'll use Middletown on my Middletown & Mystic Mines RR as an example. It's a small city with most of the space problems you're likely to encounter. It represents a town of about 25,000 people in 1925, but the techniques I'll cover can be adapted to cities of any size and era.

Most of Middletown is shown in fig. 1, and it has to share its limited space with the typical amount of track on a model railroad — too much. Adding to the problems, the track is on two levels, and the lower track bisects the area diagonally. You can see how I've placed buildings on both the upper and lower levels, so the taller ones wouldn't be too dominant. In planning Middletown I wanted to hide much of the track, make the town appear larger than it really is, and provide a reason for the railroad's large yard and roundhouse.

But for now let's put aside the problems I faced and get on with how you can create your own city. As with just about every construction project, you need a plan. A city is no exception.

CITY PLANNING

Once the space has been defined, start to lay out a city to meet your requirements. Obviously, you will need some streets, but as a general rule avoid straight ones, especially any that run perpendicular to the backdrop. It's difficult to effectively blend a perpendicular street into a backdrop, and besides, curved streets are more interesting.

To save space, streets need not be full width, particularly those that run parallel to your view. When streets are between tall buildings, you need only *suggest* that there's a full-width street separating them. The eye can be fooled into "seeing" something that is, in fact, *not* there.

Don't confine yourself to having all streets on the same level. Most cities have streets on several levels, and like curved streets these are much more interesting. However, do consider the complexity of having to adapt the base of each building to the changing levels.

Plan to put lower buildings up front, unless you are trying to achieve a special effect. I used some lower buildings in the background and placed them so they'd be seen through gaps between taller foreground structures.

Create a focal point for your city, something that will attract any viewer's eye. Once you have his attention, you can direct it to other places with structures, signs, or details. Any building can be a focal point by being particularly large, tall, or light-colored in comparison to the surrounding structures. A significant detail, such as a sign, can serve as the focal point. Middletown's focal point is a Magnuson Models five-story hotel. It's larger and lighter-colored than all the buildings around it, and it draws a viewer into the scene much as an artist directs the viewer's eye in a painting.

BACKDROP

A backdrop lends depth to your urban scene. Mine is ⅜" plasterboard (Sheetrock) nailed to 2 x 4 studs bolted to the ceiling joists. I don't have any corners in my backdrop. By scribing parallel lines about an inch apart on the *back* of the plasterboard as in fig. 2, I can form curves not only in the corners of the room but also where the wall meets the ceiling. Simply "break" the board at each scribe line, keeping the front sheet intact,

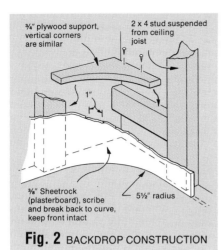

Fig. 2 BACKDROP CONSTRUCTION

so it can form a gentle curve. Figure 2 also shows how to use plywood forms to support the curved plasterboard. Tape all joints for a smooth, seamless surface.

Behind an urban scene city you'll need just a plain, sky-blue backdrop, blended at the horizon with gray, yellow, or a combination of both. I find that commercial backdrops with buildings printed on a one-dimensional surface rarely deceive the eye. Despite that, I do cut buildings from printed backdrops and cement them to my backdrop to add depth. I airbrush these cutouts with Floquil Grime to reduce their sharpness and tone down their bright colors, so they blend with the background and appear more distant.

You may want to temporarily position your three-dimensional buildings before applying any cutouts, to be sure they won't be hidden by the foreground structures. Later we'll see how three-dimensional background modeling can add even more depth to an urban scene.

MOCK-UPS

All my buildings start as cardboard mock-ups, whether the finished structure will be from a kit or scratchbuilt. The mock-ups let me see how the city will look in three dimensions, and I make them with just four walls and sometimes a roof. I usually lay out the walls on one piece of illustration board and score each corner with one stroke of a modeler's knife. Then I fold the mock-up to shape and stick it together with a piece or two of masking tape.

Try mock-ups in different locations to find the best arrangement. If your first attempt isn't pleasing, shift them around, change them, or discard them.

With very little effort you'll be able to visualize your city taking shape.

Although I use a good grade of illustration board for my mock-ups, ordinary corrugated cardboard is okay. However, I often use the mock-up as the basis of the finished model, and illustration board is better for that. I don't add windows or doors to a mock-up unless I need to see their effect, and then I just draw them on. Don't be too concerned if a mock-up won't fit between tracks — we'll see how to use air rights to get that building into the scene.

Once you are satisfied with the placement of your streets and buildings, remove the mock-ups for the installation of the streets.

CITY STREETS

I make my streets of plaster, just like any other scenery. With plaster you don't have to disguise joints, as you do with cardboard or Masonite. Figure 3 shows how I put a layer of window screen under my streets to help the plaster paving adhere. If a street climbs a hill, I support it with plywood roadbed and staple the screen to that. For level streets you can use just the screen without roadbed.

Apply the plaster as smoothly as possible to model a paved surface. When the plaster is firm but not yet fully dry, scrape the street surface with a steel rule or other straight-edged tool to peel off any high spots. After the plaster dries you may want to sand it, but don't overdo that because streets do have some minor deviations.

Next come street details — manhole covers, drains, and so forth. Use an X-acto knife or a small chisel to cut into the street surface to accept these details. Plaster can be used to patch any irregularities. While you're at it, you may want to put some plaster patches here and there to simulate street repairs.

Cracks can be drawn in with pen and India ink after the streets are painted. If you are modeling concrete-paved streets, the divisions can be scribed with an X-acto knife and a straightedge once the plaster is thoroughly dry.

I paint my asphalt streets with Floquil Grimy Black, and once that's dry I dust them with black, brown, and white chalk dust to lighten and vary the color. Whatever you do, don't leave your streets solid black! Real pavement fades with exposure to the sun and the elements until it varies from a dark to a light gray. If you've made repairs to your street, the patches should be darker since they haven't aged as long as the original paving.

To model concrete streets, substitute concrete-colored paint for Grimy Black. Most concrete surfaces become tan with age, and Floquil Concrete paint is too gray for this. Mix it with a little yellow, white, and brown to get a suitable color.

BUILDINGS

It's obvious that any city, large or small, will require many buildings. The task of making lots of structures may prompt you to switch to mountain scenery after all! However, with today's kits and materials such as styrene shapes, windows, and doors, this task has been made considerably easier.

To decide whether to use a kit, kitbash, or scratchbuild, I answer these questions:
1. Is there a kit for the building I want?
2. Will the kit fit in the space?
3. How much does the kit cost? — I don't like to buy more detail than I need.

Middletown has no out-of-the-box kit buildings. All its purchased structures are kitbashed. The remainder, about 70 percent, are scratchbuilt, but don't be misled by the amount of scratchbuilding I did. None of these buildings will ever win a prize, and most have just the minimum detail needed for an overall effect. As the fig. 4 photos show, I don't model anything that won't be seen, so my buildings have either plain, unpainted back walls or none at all.

For the money, Magnuson kits really fill the bill for city structures. They have enough detail to look good, are easy to kitbash, and represent the architecture of big-city buildings of the past. I've stretched my modeling dollar by using the extra sides, the ones you wouldn't see on the layout, in other, totally different structures. The Small & Shaw Mfg., Poli

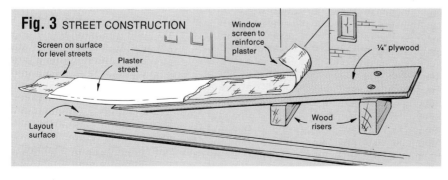

Fig. 3 STREET CONSTRUCTION

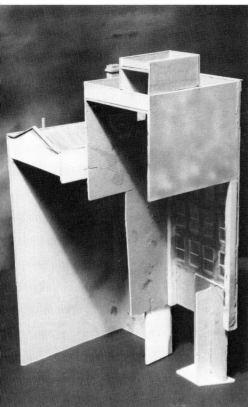

Fig. 4. CITY BUILDINGS. As you can see in the two photos at the left, Earl is not a man who likes to waste modeling effort on anything that won't be seen. These buildings have no back or side walls where they would face away from viewers, and even in front have plain walls — or none at all — below the level that will be hidden by other buildings in the foreground. The drawings below explain some of the scratchbuilding methods Earl uses.

Cutting window and door openings in styrene walls, from John Nehrich's March 1983 MODEL RAILROADER article

1. Lay out openings — segments marked "**X**" - and cut wall into horizontal strips

2. Score and snap to remove "**X**"-marked segments

3. Cement strips back together to form wall with openings

Cutting window and door openings in illustration-board walls

1. Lay out openings

2. Lay wall flat on hardboard (i.e., Masonite) backing, carefully position sharp wood chisel on edge of an opening

Illustration board on cutting board

Wood chisel

3. Rap chisel sharply with hammer to cut through illustration board, repeat around edge of each opening

Drawing window mullions on acetate glazing

Fine brush with white paint. Ferrule of brush guides along metal straightedge

¼" block glued under each end of 12" rule. Blocks raise rule above acetate so paint can't "bleed" under

Acetate taped to bench

Ice Co., and Bascom Boots buildings were made of unused sides from Magnuson's Grain Exchange, Bank, and Hotel kits.

I won't repeat the details of the many articles on kitbashing, including my "Six buildings from three" in the February 1984 MR. Just remember that if you model only the visible sides of a structure, either eliminating sides you won't see or making them from illustration board, you can use the walls left over in other buildings. The only limit is your imagination.

To find ideas for scratchbuilt structures I study old photos in books and magazines. Copying real life will almost always give your building an authentic look. Contemporary modelers need only go downtown to find ideas.

My scratchbuilding begins with sheet styrene or illustration board, and fig. 4 also shows some of my construction methods. It's easier to cut windows and doors in styrene, because you can use John Nehrich's score-and-snap method. However, with wood chisels used as in fig. 4, cutting openings in illustration board is almost as simple. Chisels come in a variety of widths, and with practice you'll be able to cut clean, square corners.

I use commercial windows and doors wherever possible. For special windows I either cast my own or draw the mullion lines onto clear acetate. To learn about home casting read Eric Bronsky's article, "Casting parts in polyester resin," in the November 1981 MR. MR Product Reviews in the April 1989 issue covered a new casting material called Alumilite.

To draw mullions I use either white ink and a pen or white paint and a fine brush, as shown in fig. 4. With light, swift strokes you can draw a clean, thin line every time.

Since most city buildings are brick, or were in 1925, we need easy ways to represent this material. For foreground buildings I laminate Holgate & Reynolds embossed vinyl brick sheet to the illustration board walls. Usually, however, I just paint the illustration board a brick color. The eye can't see a scale-size brick pattern in the smaller scales anyway, especially at a little distance, so why bother to install brick sheathing?

PAINTING AND WEATHERING

When you're "faking" brickwork with paint, color is very important. Many people think brick is red and paint models accordingly. Brick, particularly when old, is more brown than red. I mix my own brick color starting with Floquil Caboose Red and adding a little Roof Brown and Reefer Orange. The exact mixture will depend on the period you model, since newer brick is redder.

Whatever the color, the finished structure should be weathered to look authentic. City buildings soon fade in the elements, and city traffic quickly adds grime to building surfaces. I usually weather buildings with the colored chalk you can get in most artist's supply stores; orange, brown, black, and white are the colors I use most often.

Simply scrape the chalk with a single-edge razor blade to make chalk dust, mix the colors with a soft artist's brush, and brush the dry dust onto the building. In general, grime collects under the eaves and on ledges and other level surfaces, while fading occurs on surfaces exposed to the sun and elements. Areas under the eaves fade the least, since they are the most protected.

White chalk is good for fading, though I sometimes use a light color for this, such as light green to fade a green structure. A light airbrushing of Floquil Dust or Grime will also create a pleasing effect, but avoid getting this on windows.

ROOF DETAILS

Most layouts are viewed from overhead, so roof details like those in fig. 5 are important. Chimneys, skylights, roof-access hatches, ventilators, elevator shafts, water tanks, and billboards are all in this category. Since each of them comes in a number of shapes and sizes, you can have a wide variety of roof details.

Many roof details are available from Campbell, Alloy Forms, and other makers. If you can't find exactly what you need, you can easily scratchbuild most details. For example, a small square of illustration board can become a roof-access hatch. Small-diameter brass tubing can represent vent pipes. I can't overemphasize the importance of including these details, since the rooftops will be the first thing you notice if the details are missing. If you're modeling the 1950s or later, you'll want to include TV aerials on most residential buildings.

SIGNS

Of all the details you add to your city buildings, signs give you the most for your effort and money. Signs do many things. They add color, establish an era and a locale, and give buildings identity

Fig. 5. ROOF DETAILS, above. Earl stresses the need for roof details because of their prominence on most model buildings. Details on rooftops add interest and variety, and suggest that structures have more detail than is actually modeled.

Fig. 6. REVERSED SIGNS, left. Where the rear of a building will be seen in a mirror, Earl makes the back walls look like different buildings than you see from the front. He often uses reversed signs to enhance this effect. The "POOL" sign is hand-painted, but the "MANGINI" sign uses normal dry transfers on clear acetate, as explained in the text.

Fig. 7. 3-D BACKGROUND, below. This photo is a closer look than layout viewers normally get of a background scene Earl built to about half of HO scale. This is a "forced-perspective" technique for an illusion of greater depth, and it's easier to blend with foreground modeling than a two-dimensional backdrop. The N scale truck Earl is placing in the scene is a little larger than half HO scale, but it's close enough for this purpose.

Fig. 8. FRONT- VS. REAR-SURFACE MIRRORS.
The mirror on the left has its reflective silvering on its front surface, so there's no gap between an object abutting the mirror and the reflected image. Compare the ordinary rear-surface mirror on the right — with the scale rule resting on the front of the mirror you can see that there's an apparent gap equal to the thickness of the mirror glass.

and purpose. To put it simply, they add character to your city.

Signs can be applied by hand-painting, dry transfers, decals, or stencils. There are many commercial sources for signs, including Woodland Scenics, Vintage Reproductions, Finescale Miniatures, and others. Art stores offer dry-transfer alphabets of all sizes and type styles, and Sunday newspaper advertising supplements are a good source of paper signs for the contemporary era.

My article in the February 1986 MR, "Making signs for the layout," covered many sign-making methods. One technique I didn't cover is making signs in reverse, a must if you use mirrors in your scene.

The reversed Mangini sign in fig. 6 was made with dry transfers applied to clear acetate. The name "MANGINI" was made with an outline alphabet, which as the name implies has only the outline of each letter. These letters can be colored by painting the acetate between the lines. The words "MIRRORS and GLASS" are from other alphabets.

Once all the lettering was in place, I airbrushed the acetate with the background colors, covering all the lettering. Then I turned the acetate over and installed the reverse-image sign. Seen in a mirror, it reads normally.

3-D BACKGROUND

Another way to add distance is with background buildings and scenery in a scale about half that of your foreground models. Shown in fig. 7, half-scale scenery in three dimensions is easier to blend with the foreground than a flat backdrop scene and adds more depth and distance.

My half-scale background buildings are made of cardstock. I lay out all the sides of a building in one piece, including a gluing tab on one end like the tabs on paper-doll clothes. The windows and doors are drawn with pen and India ink. Then I "paint" the building with colored pencils, scribe the corners with a razor

Exquisite detail abounds in this scene, from the laundry hanging out to dry to the cat tip-toeing along the rickety railing of the back porch of the tenement buildings.

Fig. 9. MIRROR IN BACKDROP. Earl set the mirror behind Middlesex Utilities' coal yard into the backdrop, flush with the plasterboard. He concealed the mirror's top edge by spackling the joint, painting the spackling to match the backdrop, and airbrushing Floquil Reefer White along the top of the mirror.

blade, fold the building to shape, and hold it together by cementing the tab.

Scenery is also scaled down: fences, trees, autos, people, and such are smaller to blend with the half-size buildings. Distant pines can be simulated with a piece of window screening cut to look like a line of trees. Coat this screen strip with Elmer's white glue and dip it into a container of green dyed sawdust. The finished tree line goes next to the backdrop, behind the three-dimensional hills.

FOOLING THE EYE

Because we never seem to have enough space, we often have to resort to trickery to make the most of what we have. Here are some space-saving techniques.

Mirrors, properly placed, can deceive the eye into thinking there is more to a scene than actually exists. John Allen was a master at this, and his article,

"The art of using mirrors," in the December 1981 MR, is the basic reference. Malcolm Furlow also showed how to use a mirror in his article, "Sheridan, Colorado: 1927," in the July 1981 MR.

Front-surface mirrors are the best for our purposes, as you'll see in fig. 8. Front-surface mirrors are harder to find, but some outside rear-view mirrors for trucks are of this type. They have curved ends which have to be cut off or disguised, and they are usually tinted though I have not found that objectionable. I found my mirror at a local glass store for about $7.

[Edmund Scientific, phone 1-800-257-6173 (1-800-232-6677 in New Jersey), supplies front-surface mirrors in various sizes by mail. — *Ed.*]

I've used mirrors to add depth in three locations, one against the backdrop and two inside buildings. Mirrors must be

placed carefully so they won't reflect either viewers or foreground train movements. Buildings abutting a mirror must be perpendicular to the mirror surface to avoid distracting angles. The top edge of the mirror must be concealed, or the deception will not work.

A convenient way to hide the top of a mirror is with an overhead structure like an enclosed walkway. Figure 9 shows another approach I used with a mirror installed in the backdrop to "enlarge" the coal yard of Middlesex Utilities.

I modeled only half of the overhead crane, clamshell bucket, and coal pile. Reflected in the mirror, they appear whole. The coal pile also serves to keep trains passing on the track just in front of it from being reflected in the mirror. Also, I placed a mirror inside the utility's boiler house (not shown) to enlarge its interior in much the same way.

When buildings are reflected in mirrors I model their back walls to represent totally different structures than they appear to be from the front. This is where those reversed signs come in — they look normal in the reflection and fool the eye into seeing more than is really there.

Another way to get more city into a limited space is to use the railroad's "air rights" and put buildings over the tracks. Middletown is confined by track front and back, and using only the area between tracks would greatly reduce its mass.

Instead, the background structures hang over the track or are cut out to let trains pass through, as shown in fig. 10. From the front it looks as if these buildings stand on solid ground and that there's space between and behind them for the railroad. Buildings and other scenery in the foreground keep viewers from seeing the trick.

A small livery barn built as a two-sided structure, also shown in fig. 10, helps hide the background track. Because its roof and end are modeled as if it was a normal four-sided building, the eye is fooled into seeing it that way.

Similarly, the theater building has only two sides and a track passing through, bisecting it diagonally. But the roof is modeled as if the building had

Fig. 10. "AIR RIGHTS." Visitors to the Middletown & Mystic Mines RR never get to see the high-angle view in the photo below, so they don't get to see that many of Middletown's seemingly solid buildings hang over the tracks and are cut out to let trains pass through. In the photo at right, Earl has temporarily leaned a mirror against the backdrop to show how the two-sided livery barn hides a background track. Also reflected in the mirror are the overhanging roof of the theater and the backside of the billboard that keeps prying eyes from learning Middletown's secrets.

four walls, and a billboard helps disguise the narrowness of the roof and the fact that it hangs over the track. A short piece of fence on one side and a full tree on the other help keep you from seeing that the track cuts through the theater.

Speaking of trees, don't overlook them in an urban scene. Look at almost any city from a little distance and you may be surprised by the way foliage nearly hides the buildings. Trees are appropriate and effective view blocks when there's something you want to conceal.

LIGHTING

I don't put interior details in buildings unless absolutely necessary, but I do install lighting. As fig. 11 shows, a city at night is an impressive sight, and lighting up your urban scene takes only a little more effort.

Look at real buildings at night, and you'll see that the interiors will be too bright if you power the light bulbs in your buildings at their maximum rated voltage. Most buildings appear to be lit a dim yellow except, perhaps, for shopping centers. Factory windows are usually so dirty that interior light is even further diminished.

To get this look, use higher-voltage bulbs wherever possible, but power them at just a fraction of their rated voltage. The series wiring in the fig. 11 diagram is an easy way to accomplish this. Also, brightness should vary from building to building and even within buildings. The lights in a hotel lobby are much brighter than individual room lights, for example.

Use cheaper, larger bulbs when you can. Limit the grain-of-wheat bulbs to those confined areas where you have no choice. In general you'll have more flexibility in voltage with larger, higher-rated bulbs. When you do use grain-of-wheat bulbs, buy those of 12-14V ratings so you have some latitude in powering them. If, because of space constraints, you can use only the 1.5V "grain-of-sand" bulbs, it's even more important to use series wiring to limit voltage and prolong the life of these expensive bulbs.

I solder bulbs to stiff wire so I can adjust their positions for the best lighting simply by bending the wire. Of course the bulb must not be visible from the outside, and each seam of the building must be light tight. Usually you can run a bead of glue along the inside of a seam and paint it black when dry, and that will seal any crack for light.

Where you don't have interior detail, spray the windows from the inside with Krylon Matte Finish to "frost" them and hide the building's vacant look. Spraying from the inside won't dull the reflectivity of acetate or other glazing as seen from the outside. For more light in a night scene, streetlights (like my "Working streetlights" in the March 1989 MR), auto headlights, lighted signs, and other illuminated details can be added with miniature bulbs or fiber optics.

These are just a few ideas about urban modeling. Mine isn't the only way or even the best way to build a city, but I hope that what I've done in building Middletown will help you and inspire you to create your own city. ◘

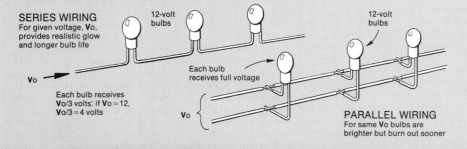

Fig. 11. LIGHTING. A city at night can be such a dramatic scene that the extra effort of lighting buildings and details is worthwhile. The series wiring shown in the drawing provides enough voltage for a realistic yellow glow and prolongs bulb life.

SERIES WIRING
For given voltage, **Vo**, provides realistic glow and longer bulb life

12-volt bulbs

V_O

Each bulb receives $V_O/3$ volts: if $V_O = 12$, $V_O/3 = 4$ volts

Each bulb receives full voltage

12-volt bulbs

V_O

PARALLEL WIRING
For same **Vo** bulbs are brighter but burn out sooner

Modeling State Line Tunnel on the NEB&W

How the Rensselaer Club added a well-known local railroad scene to its layout

Fig. 1

State line

State Line Tunnels

BY JOHN NEHRICH

*O*NE OF THE FINEST model railroads in the country is being built by the Rensselaer Model Railroad Society at Rensselaer Polytechnic Institute in Troy, N.Y. We published a cover story on the club's New England, Berkshire & Western in September 1983. Since then we've published three articles by John Nehrich describing construction methods used by the club's members: "Summit scenery on the NEB&W" (March 1984), "Two blocks of stores for the NEB&W" (September 1986), and "Tank farm at Chateaugay" (December 1987).

The NEB&W is an imaginary prototype patterned roughly after the Delaware & Hudson's line from Albany, N.Y., to Montreal, Quebec. Club members have also incorporated features of the Rutland along the New York state line, along with elements of the New York Central, Central Vermont, Boston & Maine, and the Boston & Albany.

More than fine modeling techniques, what makes the club's scenery so outstanding is the fact that they model actual scenes. One of the most striking of these is State Line Tunnel. Photos of that scene have appeared twice in MR, most recently in the September 1988 issue as the lead photo for Jeff English's article "Taconic-type 4-8-4s." Both times readers have written asking how it was modeled. Fortunately, John Nehrich had photos of the construction, which was done almost 8 years ago, and agreed to prepare the following article on how a favorite prototype scene was modeled. A more detailed explanation of backdrop construction and painting and methods for modeling foliage can be found in his "Summit scenery on the NEB&W."

State Line Tunnel as modeled by members of the Rensselaer Model Railroad Society, **left**, compared to the prototype, **above**, as it looked in the mid-1970s.

THE FIRST TRACK PLAN developed for the New England, Berkshire & Western had the main line going directly from Kendrick Mills to Schuyler, passing through a single backdrop. Eventually we decided to separate the Capital District's urban congestion from the resort area with a rural scene. So we split the backdrop into a wye configuration as shown in the track plan (fig. 1). But we still had the problem of disguising the entrance and exit of the tracks. Here we chose the traditional solution — tunnels.

RESEARCHING THE PROTOTYPE

To model an actual scene or structure requires some research. This is an aspect of the hobby that I enjoy; even if you don't you'll find that it pays dividends by helping you create a more interesting layout.

The Boston & Albany's route connects its namesake cities by meandering across the backbone of the Berkshires with many curves, grades, and cuts. Just west of the Massachusetts state line in New York the railroad tunneled through a small ridge. That structure's been named State Line Tunnel. See fig. 2.

A turn-of-the-century postcard of that site shows a double-track main line passing through a single bore. Later a third track was added through a second bore. Eventually one track was pulled up through the first tunnel, and the remaining track was centered to provide adequate clearance.

The next step was to visit the scene itself, an activity that, to paraphrase an old saying, is worth a thousand pictures. However, a piece of film has a much better memory than most of us, so once you are there, take pictures. Don't rule out

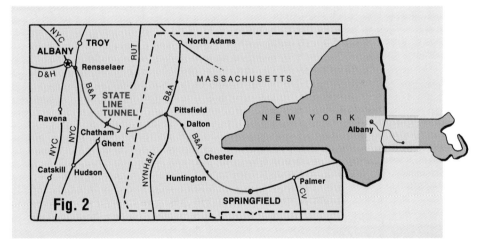

Fig. 2

Fig. 3. This aerial photo of State Line Tunnel, taken in the summer of 1978, was used in planning the model. That's a Conrail freight emerging from one of the tunnels on the old Boston & Albany line.

Construction photos by John Nehrich and Frank Lenz

Fig. 4. Left: Here's the challenge that was faced by the author and other club members: How to justify a double-track main line piercing the backdrop, which is used to separate a rural scene from a city scene. **Fig. 5. Above:** All the backdrops on the NEB&W layout are tall enough to provide ample sky in low-angle photos. Club members John Whiton (left) and Frank Lenz made quick work of attaching the Masonite to the backdrop framing.

returning there once you start work. You'll be amazed at how much you overlook the first time and suddenly find you have to know to continue.

Greg Whittle and Dick Hosmer took a couple of aerial shots because we wanted to duplicate the entire scene, not just the tunnels. Since there was a train in these shots, it was possible to calculate the distance between telephone poles, using the known length of the locomotive. Should you not be fanatical enough to buy a Cessna Piper to aid your scenery work, a more direct, accurate, and inexpensive method is to use a tape measure.

BACKDROPS

Before starting scenery we needed to build a backdrop. Unlike carpentry for the benchwork, which needs only to be strong, the backdrop must also look good.

The 2 x 4 legs support a framework of 2¼" x ¼" lath. The most difficult part was drilling into the concrete floor and ceiling to anchor the legs. Two-inch segments of L girder are used to attach the legs top

and bottom, via plastic masonry anchors. It's important to get the legs as vertical as possible in each direction. Legs are spaced every 4 feet, with one right at the joint of each 8-foot sheet of Masonite.

It's frustrating when photographing from a low angle not to have enough "sky" at the top of the shot. Thus we make the backdrop as high as possible, limited only by having to cross under the numerous pipes that serve the dorm upstairs. The bottom lath runner is as low as it can be and still clear a passing train. See figs. 5 and 6.

The bottom lath was attached first, adjusting it to a nice smooth curve. The top piece was placed against the first and marked as to leg location, so that the run and the curve were the same.

BUILDING TERRAIN

A screen-wire base. We use screen wire rather than crumpled newspaper as is usually suggested for hardshell scenery. That's not because we're reactionaries trying to revive the old system of

plaster troweled onto the screen. We've found that we can be more precise when forming the contour of hills and valleys with screen wire. So we put in a few supports, then kind of throw the screen over it and staple it in place. We attach the screen along the roadbed with lots of staples to both secure the hardshell and prevent cracks at this junction, as the wood roadbed breathes with the seasons but the hardshell doesn't.

Besides supporting the hardshell while the plaster is setting, the screen serves as a mock-up before plaster is added. During the mock-up phase you want to be able to make adjustments without having to rip out extensive carpentry. That's why I tend to clamp and not screw in the scenery risers. This makes it easy to change things by an inch here or there. Be sure you don't forget the clamps.

Forming the hardshell. For spreading out a layer of plaster, dipping paper towels into a plaster mix has two advantages. First, it's faster than laboriously troweling it onto screen. Second, the

Fig. 6. Above: After the backdrop was installed, a mock-up of the tunnel rock face was tacked in place. **Fig. 7. Right:** A frame was built for the fascia (see fig. 8). Screen wire was stapled to the roadbed and the fascia frame to support gently sloping scenery. Wood supports for the screen wire can be seen in the background.

towels become an integral part of the composite hardshell. For hardshell to develop strength it must be a true sandwiching of plaster, toweling, plaster, toweling. That's the reason merely covering the surface with towels and then pouring on plaster won't work.

I use Hydrocal for hardshell, though I think it's overrated and molding plaster or plaster of paris is adequate if the hardshell is made up of more layers. On our layout, because molding plaster and Hydrocal look identical when dumped in an unmarked container, I often confuse them and use them interchangeably. I add more layers whenever the hardshell doesn't seem strong enough, so it doesn't seem to matter.

I mix the plaster in a Pyrex meat-loaf pan because paper towels fit easily into it. Don't worry if plaster sets in the pan; just wet it and then slide it out in big slabs by pushing on it with your fingers. Never scrape with a knife or other metal object, as the plaster will adhere next time.

We use industrial-grade paper toweling that comes on a roll. I wrap several yards at a time onto a piece of 2 x 4, remove the cylinder of toweling, and cut across it on the club band saw. This yields a batch of rectangles with ragged ends. Either cut them with a saw or tear them, and don't use scissors.

The process. Arrange a large supply of cut towels, a bowl of dry plaster with a scoop, and a large container of water next to the work site. To mix the plaster thoroughly you have to use your fingers.

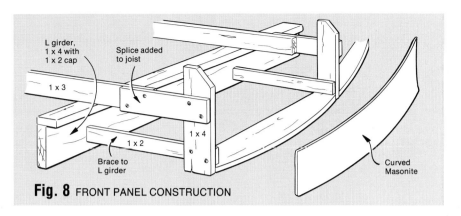

Fig. 8 FRONT PANEL CONSTRUCTION

L girder, 1 x 4 with 1 x 2 cap

Splice added to joist

1 x 3

1 x 2

1 x 4

Brace to L girder

Curved Masonite

It sounds messy — heck, it *is* messy — but it works. (Keep hand lotion around since plaster will dry out your skin.)

Put ¾" to 1" of water in the pan, dump in two or three cups of dry plaster, and start mixing. As you do so you'll get an idea of the consistency and generally will need to add more plaster. When it seems about right and you're sure the plaster has been thoroughly blended with the water, in goes the first towel. See fig. 9. This is the critical test of the consistency, as the way it covers the towel is the key.

You want the plaster to give a smooth, even coat. If the mix is too thin, the texture of the towel will show. If it's too thick, there will be gaps. The mix will thicken anyway as you work and the towels absorb water, so you may want to begin with a slightly thin mixture.

Plaster sets as a chemical reaction of water with the plaster. Unlike paint, whose setting is hastened by drying out, or white glue, which sets because it has dried, you can't delay the setting of plaster. Nor can you prolong the working time by adding more water. That simply breaks bonds that have already formed and will not reset.

Therefore, once the plaster's in place, don't pat, touch, fuss, adjust, or smooth it. *Leave it alone.* Also, don't be tempted to take the dregs at the bottom of the bowl and smear them on the wet scenery.

After 10 or 15 minutes the plaster will become warm. This is a sign of a successful hardshell application. Once it's begun to cool you may handle it. Even when totally set, the plaster is strongest when dry. If you need to do any surgery,

Fig. 9. Left: John Nehrich, the author, is shown dipping paper towel strips in a soupy plaster mix. Next he'll drape the towels over the screen-wire base. **Fig. 10. Above right:** As plaster-soaked paper towels are applied over the screen wire, the basic hardshell terrain begins to take shape.

Fig. 11. With more of the area covered with hardshell, the final look of the scene emerges. **Fig. 12. Above:** The rock molds were made from coal chunks.

Fig. 13. Above: The first castings that the author made were used to line the tunnels. Fig. 14. Below: Next, a few castings for the prominent outcropping between the two bores were selected.

Fig. 15. Above: Separate castings were blended together to form the right bore. At this point the decision was made to cut the wood frame so the left bore could be set back like the prototype. Fig. 16. Below: This is what the completed tunnels looked like before doing any carving. For many modelers this look would be satisfactory.

first rewet the plaster. Figures 10 and 11 show how the appearance of the area changes as more and more of the screen wire is covered with hardshell.

When confronted with a vertical or nearly vertical surface, I don't try to add the hardshell in one step — the plaster-laden towels will slide merrily down the screen. Instead, I start with a very thin mix. Towels dipped in this stay put. Once dry, they will absorb water from the next layer, water that would lubricate the sliding. If the plaster dries out before it sets, wet it again and the setting will continue unharmed.

If you're adding new hardshell to old, either first rewet the old to prevent it from soaking up the water from the new hardshell or squirt on some water after you've added the new layer. Both methods work, though I prefer the second. I've found that no matter how much water I add, more is needed in a few minutes.

After applying several layers to an area I let the hardshell set. Then I rap certain spots with my knuckles. The sound tells if everything's *sound*.

ROCK CASTINGS

Making the molds. I like casting plaster rocks more than anything in the hobby. The first step is either buying or making the molds. If you make your own out of liquid latex (Mountains in Minutes is a popular brand), select rocks similar to the prototype you're modeling. We used coal because it's sedimentary and finely detailed, matching the texture of the rocks around State Line Tunnel.

Begin by washing the rock masters with soapy water. While the rock is still wet, brush on a layer of latex, as shown in fig. 12, and let it dry — no catalyst, hardener, mixing or measuring is required. Use a cheap brush to apply the latex since no matter how diligent you are in washing it out after each coat, it will soon be mummified in rubber.

When the first coat is dry (you can tell because it becomes clear), add another until five or six have built up. Next, embed a layer of cheesecloth or strips of gauze in the wet latex. Follow this with another coat or two of latex. Let the mold dry thoroughly, then peel it off the master.

Casting methods. There are two commonly used techniques of applying rock castings. The first is to slap them on while still wet and in the mold. This has the advantage of being fast and, because the castings are still pliable, of conforming to the scenery contours.

The other method involves building them up after setting. This offers more control: I can prop up each casting in turn, shift it to find the best position, and compare it to other castings to see how they'll fit together and whether they'll capture the actual scene. It would also seem better for the stratified rock we were modeling, where the rock face changes direction in square steps.

FITTING ROCK CASTINGS

The first castings went to line the walls of the tunnels (fig. 13). I thought I could make the tunnel roofs removable and thereby have access to color the rocks and ballast the tracks. On other tunnels I've made a U-shaped liner by draping a large mold over a former (a 2 x 4 on edge, for example) and smearing on a thick mix of plaster. The bending of the rock strata wasn't discernible in the dark of the tunnel, and we managed to color and ballast with the liner installed.

On this one I added flat castings on top of the walls and wound up with large gaps, because the top of the walls were so irregular. The ceiling was also too high. Not only were we going to have to color and ballast through the tunnel ends, but more plastering of the ceiling was needed. However, inserting my arm to work cut off my vision. (How do they ever manage tonsillectomies, anyway?) Puzzled, I continued work on the exterior faces.

I let this problem sit for a while. It didn't matter what the roofs looked like, but the gaps had to be fixed. I put globs of plaster on my fingertips, reached inside, and smeared them into any gaps I could feel. The fingers served as both a tool and a sensing device. Afterwards I chipped off the low hanging blobs.

Rock faces. The major element of this scene is the rock faces. I was a little hesitant about starting it because it promised to be a long, drawn-out effort of trying to match the prototype as closely as possible.

One Friday evening as I was playing around with castings I noticed that one resembled the prominent formation between the two actual bores. That got me started, and the castings seemed to fly together. I kept the coffeepot going and by sunrise had the whole face done. I even remembered to take time to photograph my progress, as you'll see by referring to figs. 14 and 15.

Securing castings. Attaching castings to the hardshell is easy. The water-stealing ability of the old plaster instantly firms up the "mortar" you're using to attach the castings. Sometimes interlocking with other castings is enough to hold the new one in place. Then you merely trowel plaster into the joints and begin shaping it. Most of the time, however, the casting doesn't stay put. Then I hold it or prop it up and use a few dabs of plaster to tack-weld it. Later I work more plaster into the joints.

It's possible to erode the wet plaster in the joints with a spray of water to remove unnatural marks and swirls. This is ideal for a rock outcropping when the rocks peek out from a layer of soil. But in our scene the rock is uninterrupted,

Fig. 17

Cut strata with utility knife

Undercut strata with chisel blade

Pry sections of plaster with blade

Plaster fractures in front of blade

Undercut strata

Shadows

so the mortar has to look like a continuation of the casting. Try to continue the strata lines across the joints so they don't draw attention to themselves.

CARVING ROCK

The tunnel face was probably close enough when the rock castings were installed and blended together (fig. 16), but I got ambitious and extensively recarved much of it. Why didn't I just start with blank plaster and carve that? I didn't because the castings provide a lot of detail in areas that aren't as important to capturing the character of the scene.

Actually, instead of carving away rock, I concentrated on carving *in* shadows. This method worked particularly well for modeling this prototype because the rockwork is mostly undercut. Occasionally I would break through the casting, but it was easy to trowel on more plaster and keep carving.

There's no mystery about what you're trying to achieve. Pick up a piece of plaster, snap it, and look at the resulting surface. That's what you want to duplicate when carving rocks.

For this I use two tools: a utility knife to carve in strata lines and an X-acto chisel blade used sideways to remove plaster in bulk. Use the blade to pry off plaster rather than slicing it. The result looks more natural because you're imitating the natural process of frost prying off rock along natural fracture lines (fig. 17). Of course in the case of State Line Tunnel blasting powder did that!

ROCK COLORING

Traditionally rockwork has been colored with stains. That's okay for individual castings, but it destroys the hard-won continuity of a wall composed of castings and carved-in fill. The plaster absorbs more or less stain depending on how porous it is, and the more stain absorbed the stronger the color. On a patchwork wall like this one the castings are more porous than the plaster of the surrounding joints, which got compacted when squeezed into

the gaps. If you stain the rockwork, the joints will be conspicuous because of their absence of color.

Instead, I color the plaster rockwork the same way I color other scenery. I begin by applying a base coat of latex paint, followed by washes to weather and mottle the surface. This is easier to control than stain, which may turn out to be too strong. With my technique the base color seals the pores, rendering the whole surface equally impervious to color. Consequently, washes only gently add color. If you're dissatisfied, just repaint the surface with the base color.

For this scene I painted the rocks an off-white latex, followed by dark washes. The strong photofloods tend to wash out what is seen as acceptable color under ambient lighting.

ADDING FOLIAGE

Coloring the plaster. First paint the white plaster so none of it will show. I used a dark brown latex house paint on all the plaster except the rock faces. This sufficed for the depths of the forest, but in more open areas I followed by sprinkling on real dirt. Figure 18 shows how the scene looked at this point.

I added foliage from the portals towards the woods, but that order's not vital. Elsewhere trees went in first, and grass was added as part of the final detailing.

When the dirt had dried, I puddled undiluted white glue in areas about 2" square and planted clumps of fibers cut from patches of synthetic materials, such as fake fur or material sold for making fishing lures. This fishing lure material comes in more natural colors.

Fig. 18. Top: Before the trees and foliage were added, all the hardshell terrain was painted with brown latex paint. **Fig. 19. Middle:** This weed, which is called St. John's Wort, was used for making most of the deciduous trees on the layout. **Fig. 20. Bottom:** The author drilled all the holes for the trees at one time so the mess could easily be cleaned up before he planted the trees.

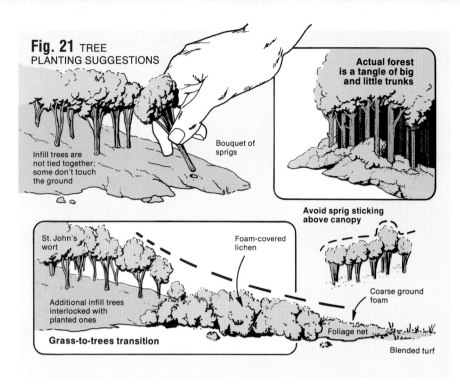

Fig. 21 TREE PLANTING SUGGESTIONS

Infill trees are not tied together; some don't touch the ground

Bouquet of sprigs

Actual forest is a tangle of big and little trunks

Avoid sprig sticking above canopy

St. John's wort

Foam-covered lichen

Additional infill trees interlocked with planted ones

Grass-to-trees transition

Coarse ground foam

Foliage net

Blended turf

Net bushes. I spread foliage netting around the perimeter above the portals, then sprayed it heavily with hair spray. [The brand of foliage netting the author used is no longer available. AMSI — Architectural Model Supply Inc., P. O. Box 3497, San Rafael, CA 94914 — has a similar tree cover material that's sold through hobby shops. — *Ed.*]

I sprinkled on blended turf from Woodland Scenics next. Toward the edge of the woods I added the coarser foam we use to coat other foliage. This blurred the transition from low-lying bushes into the woods. Patches of the foliage-net bushes were also worked into the grassy patch between the tracks.

MAKING TREES

Our basic deciduous tree is made from a weed we pick that's commonly called St. John's Wort. A sample is shown in fig. 19. This is a standard feature of architect's models (even those in scales that are smaller than HO) because it has such fine texture.

St. John's Wort seems to be everywhere, not surprising for a plant that prefers the poorly nourished soil found in pastures and along cinder-filled railroad embankments. It grows in bushes that are about 3 feet high and have pinkish-white blossoms in the summer. We gather our weeds late in the fall, when the whole bush has a faint reddish tinge. Picked dry, they require no glycerine or other preservative.

At its peak, the fall foliage around here is so spectacular as to be unbelievable enough in the real world, let alone as an attempted model. Done accurately, an HO fall scene would look too bright and toylike. That's why we model early autumn. Besides making the layout look more realistic, the subdued colors don't draw attention from the railroad.

PLANTING TREES

Drilling a hole for a tree kicks up a lot of plaster dust. Therefore, before planting any we try to drill enough ¼" and ⅜" holes in an area to take care of all the trees we'll want and more. As fig. 20 shows, the hardshell winds up looking like Swiss cheese.

Making each tree is a simple process. First gather a bouquet of sprigs and break off the excess lower lengths. Next, dunk it in diluted white glue and roll it in the foam. We use AMSI fine and medium grades of foam, mixing various shades together in shoe boxes so the shades differ from box to box. Now insert it in one of the holes.

I prefer to make up each tree on the spot and plant it while still wet. I don't tie the bouquet together, but instead rely on the hole in the scenery to hold the tree together. The wet glue on the branches runs down and secures the tree to the ground.

A real forest is a tangle of big and little trunks. To achieve this in the interior of our woods we use the branches of the St. John's Wort not as trunks but to raise the foam-coated blossoms up at treetop. Thus the more sprigs in the bouquet, the faster the hills can be wooded.

I gather enough sprigs for a press fit in the ¼" and ⅜" holes. Once an area has enough planted trees, others can be added without sticking them in the holes or even having the twigs touch the ground. Toward the edge of the woods, where more can be seen, extra care is taken in planting. For example, foam-covered lichen is poked into the forest to continue the uninterrupted sweep of green from ground level to treetop (see fig. 21 for suggestions on planting trees).

CONCLUSION

Well, that's the story behind State Line Tunnel. It's a recognizable scene that never fails to win compliments from visitors to the NEB&W. Even though we take pride in remarks about the nice modeling, the best is overhearing someone say, "That looks *exactly* like State Line Tunnel on the old Boston & Albany." ✿

The Rensselaer Society's NEB&W layout is open to visitors every Saturday afternoon. A $3 donation is suggested. Call (518) 276-2764 for information.

Fig. 22. The Rensselaer Club's model of State Line Tunnel is a dead ringer for the prototype.

Rock-fill crib walls

An alternative to sheer rock faces and brick retaining walls

BY BILL LORENCE

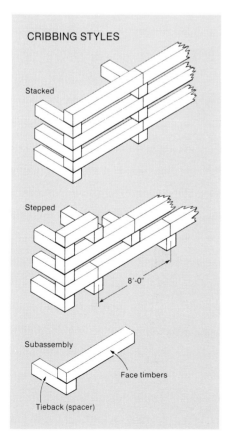

CRIBBING STYLES

Stacked

Stepped

8'-0"

Subassembly

Face timbers

Tieback (spacer)

ONE of the major problem areas for modelers is how to construct scenery when two tracks at different vertical elevations are too close together to permit a sloping hillside. For background scenery an overly steep hill is not objectionable, but in the foreground a vertical cliff is acceptable only in a mountainous setting. Stone and brick retaining walls are overused in this type of situation.

One solution that I have used is an open-face, rock-fill crib wall. These are very common in rolling country and rocky areas. The modeling procedure is not difficult, and the result is visually very pleasing. I installed one such crib wall with a rock embankment at my coal transfer tipple as shown in the photograph above.

My crib walls are built up of timbers cut from match sticks. I cut them approximately 8 scale feet long and stain them before assembly. Campbell bridge ties will also work well, but I prefer the rustic appearance produced by uneven match sticks. Aside from that, matches are cheaper and can first be used to light a stove or fire.

Decomposed granite makes excellent rubble fill and embankments. What is particularly appealing about this material is that it looks — and is — natural.

To grade the material I use a common flour sifter, which can be found in the housewares section of any hardware store. My rubble fill is the waste left over from sifting out HO ballast-sized stone from crushed granite. I use the ballast size to fill in between the larger rubble pieces. The top is dusted with a mix of both. Other materials that can be used for backfill are commercial model rock or natural materials such as sand or sifted dirt right from the garden.

The ties can be stacked or stepped as shown in the accompanying drawing. Stacked cribs are the type more commonly used. Sometimes a combination is used to suit the topography of the area. Such is the case in my example: stepped at the top, and stacked at the bottom.

To facilitate handling of the timbers, I make subassemblies of short tieback and face timbers. In one evening, while watching television, I easily glued up all the pieces I needed for this project. Using white glue I start by assembling three or four rows of timbers. When the glue has dried, I backfill the cribbing with rubble and stone and affix the fill with a mixture of 50 percent white glue, 50 percent water, and a few drops of a liquid detergent. I alternate, adding a lift of three or four rows and backfilling until I get the correct height.

The whole project is fast, simple, and scenically effective. ✿

Downtown Milwaukee on the

Using photo posters for a distinctive backdrop

BY JIM KELLY
COLOR PHOTOS BY A. L. SCHMIDT

OVER THE DOZEN or so years of its existence, the HO scale Milwaukee, Racine & Troy (MODEL RAILROADER's club railroad) has undergone many changes. Among these was the installation of a freestanding backdrop on the Milwaukee section, which resulted in the scenic challenge shown in fig. 1. Already in place was the Port Marquette Yard, the MR&T's eastern terminus at Milwaukee. We had also roughed in the canal, and the tanker *Linn H. Westcott* was already plying its plywood waters (sorry about that). Plans called for a bridge across the end of the canal to hide its junction with the backdrop and a mirror under the bridge to make the canal look as though it continued into the distance.

Erecting the backdrop had left some complicated trackage on the far side of the canal inaccessible, and it had to come out. Any new track in that area would have to be very simple and 99.99 percent derailment-free. Also, club members wanted a passenger station for our Amtrak patrons. Beyond that, the sky (represented by blue-painted Masonite) was the limit, just so that what we ended up with looked something like Milwaukee.

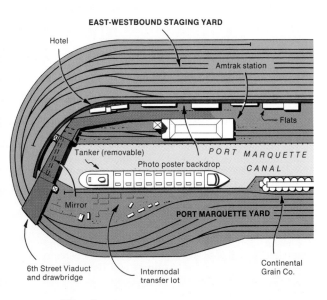

Fig. 1 DOWNTOWN MILWAUKEE ON THE MR&T

MR&T

MILWAUKEE UNION STATION

719
Milwaukee, Racine & Troy

MR 17
Milwaukee, Racine & Troy 902

MR

Milw

Fig. 2. Here's one of four shots of Milwaukee's skyline we had converted to Kodak Poster Prints and used for our city backdrop. If you look through the viewer of a 35-mm camera and see scenes with the same relative sizes, they should work out for an HO backdrop.

THE PHOTO POSTER BACKDROP

"If it's gonna look like Milwaukee, it oughta be Milwaukee," I figured, so rather than use a generic city backdrop, I decided to try a blown-up photo of Milwaukee itself. After trying several local photo houses and the newspaper for something appropriate, I decided to take my own skyline pictures, a job that turned out to be easier said than done.

First of all, there was considerable debate about the angle from which the backdrop photos should be taken. The layout is low, about belt-buckle high, so should I take backdrop photos that would look natural when viewing the layout or when photographing it from low angles? This argument has come up many times in club affairs, and in the end we've usually compromised with something halfway between. Next time we'll build the layout higher.

I finally decided on the higher angle and took 35-mm slides (see fig. 2) from the roof of the Milwaukee Public Museum, all the while being closely supervised by a security guard. The camera was on a tripod, so I could take one picture and then swing to one side with no change in elevation or angle to take another. I took two shots at one location, then moved to the other end of the roof and took another set of two.

Frankly I was amazed at how well the resulting photos could be fitted together, particularly as I really wasn't thinking about using them intact when I shot them. The four photos took in almost 180 degrees of the scene in front of me. If you take the same approach you can be more conscious of where the joints between your shots come and get more backdrop for your money.

A few more thoughts on your photos. Obviously you need a nice day, and you should choose a time of day when the sun will be at your back. Based on my experience, you can count on getting about 8 to 10 feet of backdrop at one location.

Finding good photo vantage points probably won't be easy. Supervisors of tall buildings don't want people on the roofs or shooting out open windows. (The museum owed us a favor, but ordinarily could not honor such a request.) Your best bet might be to look for good hillside or public bridge locations.

To see how well the slides would work, I projected them on the backdrop with a zoom lens, making the image smaller and larger until it looked right. Also, I placed some HO structures and equipment in front of the projected slides to get a feel for size. Armed with the enlargement ratios I'd figured out, I went to several color photo shops to see about having prints made. Soon I learned the cost would be about $85 per print, too much, I feared, to make the technique useful to most of our readers.

To the rescue came Kodak's Poster Prints. You can order these from almost any place that deals in Kodak film and processing. The poster size is 20″ x 30″, and the cost is about $14. The quality is not as good as what you'd get in more expensive custom-made prints, but it's plenty good enough for use as a model railroad backdrop. The one big disadvantage is that you can't specify the amount of enlargement you want. Kodak makes the prints full-frame of the slides you give them, so all my calculating had gone for naught. As it turned out, though, the Kodak posters came quite close to the ideal percentages I had figured.

The best way to solve the percent of enlargement problem is to take it into account when first photographing the scenes. If your shots have about the same relative proportions as the one shown in fig. 2, you'll be about right for HO. To accomplish this you need to be about one city block from the closest buildings, provided you're using a standard lens.

In the end, getting the proper distance between camera and subject is probably one of those things it's easy to worry about excessively. I discovered that sizes of the backdrop buildings don't matter much, *as long as* they aren't noticeably larger than would be correct for the scale being modeled.

I suspect that this poster-print technique doesn't promise much for N scale, as you'd have to be too far from the buildings to get sufficiently sharp images. For N scale I'd take the same slides, but have drugstore-variety 8″ x 10″ prints made.

MOUNTING THE BACKDROP

Before cementing the poster prints to the backdrop I taped them up with masking tape to get a feel for where they should go, as shown in fig. 3. (At this point I realized the simplest and best way to use them was to trim the edges and butt them together in the same order I'd shot them.)

As shown in fig. 4, I mounted the backdrop photos with rubber cement, using techniques usually used with commercial paper backdrops. I trimmed off the sky with a steel rule and a hobby knife fitted with a no. 11 X-acto blade. This turned out to be time-consuming but interesting, as I would recognize buildings and distant shapes as I went along — "Oh sure, that's the Pfister Tower." Rather than cut around every ventilator and tower atop the buildings, I cut most of the rooflines off straight.

I had to fudge and trim where photos butted together and discovered that sides of tall buildings work best for making these seams. Also, the verticals in the photos weren't parallel (nor can they be in any photo), so I had to pick out the most important vertical element near the middle of each photo and make it vertical, letting the others fall where they would. (Our artists call this process "justifying the verticals.")

After the backdrop shots were trimmed I turned them over and lightly taped them together with masking tape behind the seams. Next, I used small pieces of masking tape to trial-fit them to the Masonite. Once I was happy with their location, I outlined them lightly with a pencil so I'd be able to mount them in the same place later.

I painted the area where the backdrops were to go (as well as the backs of the prints) with rubber cement, then let both surfaces dry. After about 20 minutes I mounted the prints to the backdrop using the contact-cement method. When the surfaces touch they grab, so the positioning must be right the first time. If I had it to do over, I'd use sheets of wrapping paper or newspaper behind the backdrops so I could position them carefully before pulling the paper away and gradually attaching the scenes.

Once the backdrops were in position I rolled them down firmly with a hard rubber roller (usually called a brayer in art supply stores). Then I used a rubber-cement pick to pull away the exposed cement. (If you can't find such a pick, you can make one by pouring out some rubber cement and letting it dry.)

The photo paper is considerably heavier than commercial backdrop paper and tends to curl and pull away along the edges with time. Where this happened I reattached it with Walthers Goo.

On a small layout it might be practical to use Kodak's Poster Prints exclusively, though on a layout the size of the MR&T it would be a major undertaking and not worth it. We've found that there's no problem in using the photo posters and commercial backdrops together. Viewers accept the transition without any problem, if it occurs unobtrusively behind a large building or a flat.

Black-and-white photos: Gordon Odegard

Fig. 3. MOCKING UP THE SCENE
Above: Before cutting up our Poster Prints we tacked them up with masking tape to study the possibilities. A cardboard mock-up of the station helped in studying the relationships between the backdrop and the foreground modeling. Eventually four prints were used.

Fig. 4. MOUNTING THE PHOTO BACKDROP
Above left: The photo sky was trimmed away with a sharp X-acto knife.
Above middle: Thinned rubber cement was brushed on the backdrop.

Above right: Rubber cement was also painted on the Poster Print backs.
Below left: A hard rubber roller was used to press the photo paper down.
Below right: Excess cement was picked off with a rubber-cement pick.

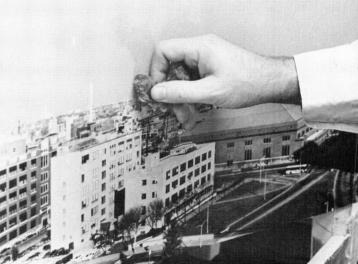

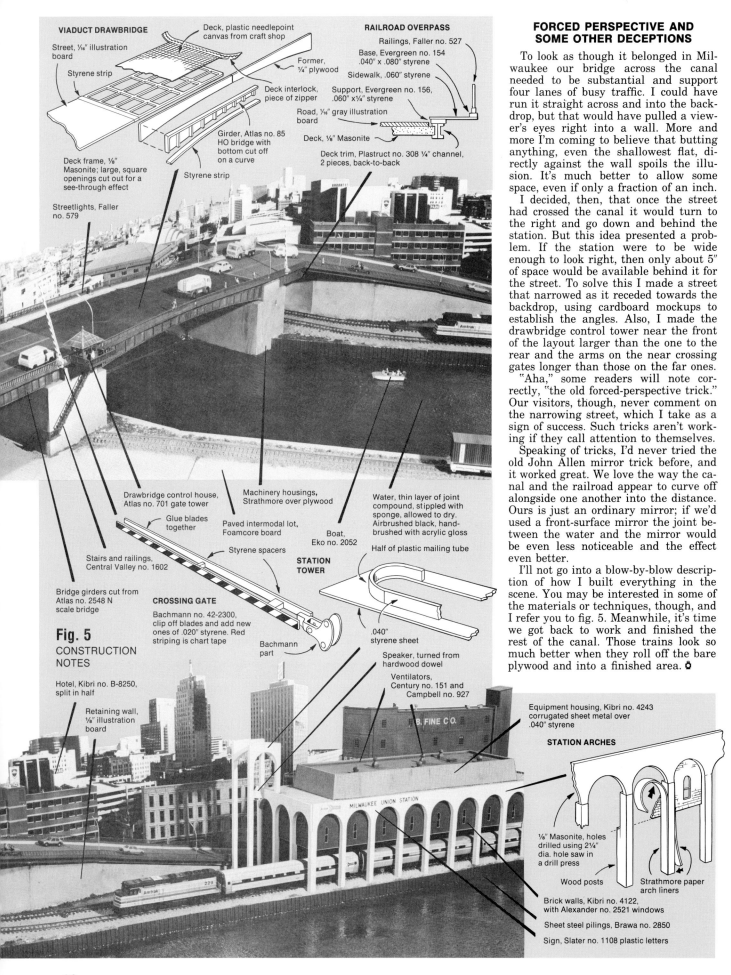

FORCED PERSPECTIVE AND SOME OTHER DECEPTIONS

To look as though it belonged in Milwaukee our bridge across the canal needed to be substantial and support four lanes of busy traffic. I could have run it straight across and into the backdrop, but that would have pulled a viewer's eyes right into a wall. More and more I'm coming to believe that butting anything, even the shallowest flat, directly against the wall spoils the illusion. It's much better to allow some space, even if only a fraction of an inch.

I decided, then, that once the street had crossed the canal it would turn to the right and go down and behind the station. But this idea presented a problem. If the station were to be wide enough to look right, then only about 5″ of space would be available behind it for the street. To solve this I made a street that narrowed as it receded towards the backdrop, using cardboard mockups to establish the angles. Also, I made the drawbridge control tower near the front of the layout larger than the one to the rear and the arms on the near crossing gates longer than those on the far ones.

"Aha," some readers will note correctly, "the old forced-perspective trick." Our visitors, though, never comment on the narrowing street, which I take as a sign of success. Such tricks aren't working if they call attention to themselves.

Speaking of tricks, I'd never tried the old John Allen mirror trick before, and it worked great. We love the way the canal and the railroad appear to curve off alongside one another into the distance. Ours is just an ordinary mirror; if we'd used a front-surface mirror the joint between the water and the mirror would be even less noticeable and the effect even better.

I'll not go into a blow-by-blow description of how I built everything in the scene. You may be interested in some of the materials or techniques, though, and I refer you to fig. 5. Meanwhile, it's time we got back to work and finished the rest of the canal. Those trains look so much better when they roll off the bare plywood and into a finished area. ☒

VIADUCT DRAWBRIDGE

Street, ¹⁄₁₆″ illustration board

Styrene strip

Deck frame, ⅛″ Masonite; large, square openings cut out for a see-through effect

Streetlights, Faller no. 579

Deck, plastic needlepoint canvas from craft shop

Former, ¼″ plywood

Deck interlock, piece of zipper

Girder, Atlas no. 85 HO bridge with bottom cut off on a curve

Styrene strip

RAILROAD OVERPASS

Railings, Faller no. 527

Base, Evergreen no. 154 .040″ x .080″ styrene

Sidewalk, .060″ styrene

Support, Evergreen no. 156, .060″ x ¼″ styrene

Road, ¹⁄₁₆″ gray illustration board

Deck, ⅛″ Masonite

Deck trim, Plastruct no. 308 ¼″ channel, 2 pieces, back-to-back

Drawbridge control house, Atlas no. 701 gate tower

Glue blades together

Machinery housings, Strathmore over plywood

Paved intermodal lot, Foamcore board

Styrene spacers

Boat, Eko no. 2052

Water, thin layer of joint compound, stippled with sponge, allowed to dry. Airbrushed black, hand-brushed with acrylic gloss

Half of plastic mailing tube

STATION TOWER

Stairs and railings, Central Valley no. 1602

Bridge girders cut from Atlas no. 2548 N scale bridge

Fig. 5
CONSTRUCTION NOTES

CROSSING GATE

Bachmann no. 42-2300, clip off blades and add new ones of .020″ styrene. Red striping is chart tape

Bachmann part

.040″ styrene sheet

Speaker, turned from hardwood dowel

Ventilators, Century no. 151 and Campbell no. 927

Hotel, Kibri no. B-8250, split in half

Retaining wall, ⅛″ illustration board

Equipment housing, Kibri no. 4243 corrugated sheet metal over .040″ styrene

STATION ARCHES

⅛″ Masonite, holes drilled using 2¼″ dia. hole saw in a drill press

Wood posts

Strathmore paper arch liners

Brick walls, Kibri no. 4122, with Alexander no. 2521 windows

Sheet steel pilings, Brawa no. 2850

Sign, Slater no. 1108 plastic letters

It's a Styrofoam sky!

Foam insulation board for photo backdrops

BY LOU SASSI
PHOTOS BY THE AUTHOR

Lou photographed the city of Adams on his HO B&M West Hoosic Div. layout before (above) and after he'd included a Styrofoam sky backdrop (below). The improvement is plain.

Have you ever stumbled upon that perfect photo location on your layout only to find that for one reason or another the background ruined the picture? Nothing can be more distracting in a model photo than a concrete cellar wall or a wall full of life-size paraphernalia looming in the distance. Well, help is as close as your nearest lumberyard.

One evening while wandering around Bill McChesney's HO layout, camera in hand, I inquired whether he had something to temporarily prop up behind a photo spot to give the impression of a distant sky. Bill uses extruded polystyrene insulation for a scenery base. This material is made by the Dow Chemical Co., comes in 2 x 8-foot sheets 1" thick, and is a sky-blue color. Bill quickly grabbed a 2 x 4-foot scrap and held it behind the scene to be photographed. It worked perfectly!

INSTANT SKY

Realizing the potential of this "instant sky," I took home another 2 x 4-foot piece and in about half an hour globbed on some clouds with a sponge and a bit of white and gray latex house paint. (Don't use anything else!) If you also prefer clouds, there is an excellent article on the subject by John Nehrich ("Summit scenery on the NEB&W") in the March 1984 issue of MR. Next, I found an artist's tripod in my basement, set the Styrofoam on it behind the city of Adams, and took a photo. In no time at all I had eliminated a background of picture frames and shelves.

Styrofoam has several nice features. It's cheap — about $4 a sheet. It doesn't require painting, and the clouds are optional. It's extremely light: a 2 x 4-foot sheet weighs less than a pound, enabling you to hang it from the ceiling with light string or thread and pushpins if you'd rather not use a tripod. Once you've finished shooting, just slide it away in a corner for future use or, if you decide to do foam scenery, make a mountain out of it. ✿

The backdrop can be put on a tripod and set behind a module for taking photos indoors or out.

Modeling a mood

How to use
fine art principles
to make our model
scenes more effective

The author has built a convincing O scale model of Edward Hopper's famous 1942 painting *Nighthawks*

BY JOHN ARMSTRONG
PHOTOS BY THE AUTHOR

DOES FINE ART have anything to teach those of us who call ourselves model railroaders? First off, what do we mean by "fine art"? Definitions, controversial after centuries of learned discussion, still sound pretty vague to us mechanics, but the thrust of one found in a current dictionary is that fine art "seeks and is judged by its success in creating beauty or meaningfulness."

Well, the word "beauty" might seem to exclude turntables, coal docks, and many other of our essentials. But we may have more luck with "meaningfulness," which implies that affecting the way the viewer feels can also raise an object in value. Sure enough, we find that the most widely appreciated paintings are not always those that are most correctly proportioned and detailed or otherwise most directly representative of the subject. Rather, they go beyond accurate representation to create a mood that somehow makes the viewer feel present and involved.

HOW CAN IT GET ANY BETTER?

Now, of course, to many of us the sight of a train running smoothly through a nicely modeled scene is enough to create a thoroughly pleasurable feeling; in fact, judging from the situation on lots (perhaps a majority) of O scale layouts, unrelieved plywood terrain is no barrier to euphoria if the trains themselves are finely crafted, long, and frequent. If they're also of the right vintage, class, and color, the feeling is so intense that it's difficult to see any room for further enhancement. Is there something *beyond* ecstasy?

Still, there may be some fine art techniques that we can adopt to make our scenes even more effective. We could put ourselves right into the mood of a hot afternoon on the east side of Raton Pass or a misty sunrise on the curving shore of Narragansett Bay and *then* run a train through the scene — WOW!

NO PICASSO, MUCHACHOS

So, if we weren't already 284 kits behind in our modeling, what we could do would be to go to art school, learn the principles of composition, light, color, painting, and starvation, and go on from there. But rather than starting from scratch, I suggest we try fitting our trains into scenes based on masterpieces whose widespread appeal has demonstrated, over the decades or centuries, that they have that certain something!

Our sources *are* somewhat circumscribed. For example, various works of "Abstract Impressionist" persuasion are not compatible with even the least successful examples of our railroad modeling. And as for "Surrealism," well, Salvador Dali may be a superdetailer, but the odd and illogical scenes he paints scarcely resemble what we find on any of our layouts.

So, we zero in on the "Realists" — those whose aim is to capture the way actual objects and scenes appear to the viewer. Right off, we find kindred spirits! From the early Renaissance on, these masters haven't hesitated to "improve on nature" by selecting or, if necessary, inventing appealing subjects and then combining and arranging them to strengthen the final effect (interest, thoughtfulness, if not outright pleasure) on the viewer.

It's taken a few centuries to broaden the field of "proper" art subjects from religious and heroic figures, idyllic landscapes, and front-door cityscapes to include most of the artifacts essential in a railroad context. In this connection, we're likely to think first of the works of a group of American painters ("The Eight," sometimes less reverently referred to as the "Ashcan School") who in the early years of this century featured previously off-limit backyard elements and less-than-affluent areas in their cityscapes.

ANGLES, SHADOWS, AND PEOPLE

We should be able to find subjects related to our interests. Are there useful principles we can identify?

We must probably reject or confine to the background most of the innovative representational methods of the late-1900s Impressionists — the feeling of a squinty look at a realistically dirty Big Boy at full speed might well be best captured by multi-hued splotches of pigment, but we need a paint job that can also stand close-up scrutiny, day or night, on the road or under the lights of a station or engine terminal. Nevertheless, many of the most respected masterpieces, before and after the time of the Impressionists, have been characterized by approaches we in "mainstream" (as opposed to diorama) model railroading tend to neglect:

● The angular perspectives of a close-up viewpoint.

● The interplay of light and shade.

● The presence (or at least the suggestion) of people.

Walk-in track plans and the gradual rise of layout base heights over the years have brought trains and accompanying structures closer up. As discussed in the accompanying sidebar, there are limiting factors associated with the way we see things that have to be considered, but — as the makers of dioramas have demonstrated, not only by running off with all the photographic prizes but by impressing the rest of us with the realism of their scenes — we should be able

to put ourselves into our scenes a lot more than we have typically done.

As a steady diet, of course, we can't tolerate shade because some of the most fascinating parts of our models — most notably, steam locomotive valve gear, although these days some modelers manage to get almost as excited about subtle differences in Blomberg diesel truck details — need illumination relatively free of shadows to be fully appreciated. Nevertheless, a dominant characteristic of Rembrandt's art is his "chiaroscuro" approach that captures the character of a subject in terms of degrees of contrast between light and shadow.

By providing effective lighting to simulate both sunshine and night we should be able to double the artistic impact of a model without going through the agony of building a second one. Sounds like a good deal, even though the time required to install, adjust, and maintain such lighting is far from trivial!

START WITH A MASTERPIECE

In trying with our more ordinary skills to retain the impact of a master painter while translating his art into three dimensions within one segment of a model railroad, we might as well start with an example widely regarded as one of the masterpieces of the twentieth century. To come down to cases, a painting that combines striking composition and contrasts in lighting with just four figures (of "late steam era" vintage, yet!) to invoke an intense, often eery mood is Edward Hopper's 1942 work *Nighthawks*.

We should be aware that there are no direct railroad references in this particular painting. Such references, ranging from track to Pullman interiors, do appear in several of Hopper's other paintings. Even so, the mood set by *Nighthawks* is more than slightly reminiscent

of the lonely, all-night occupations and occasions that are inseparable from railroading. That's why a train nearby really wouldn't be out of place.

Let's see what we're up against in trying to reproduce Hopper's mood within the confines of a "typical" in-business but only partially scenicked layout: specifically, mine. The fact that this segment (fig. 1) has been in existence for only nine years less than Hopper's classic is a jolting reminder of just how leisurely my pace of completion has been.

Practically, we should stick to areas not too far from eye level. Although striking second-story-window or more distant bird's-eye viewpoints are not uncommon in Hopper's works, he painted this picture as it would be seen by a lanky observer (he was 6'-5" tall) standing in the street. Similarities in the composition of our scene and that of its "prototype" will be most obvious if viewed from approximately the same elevation.

We want the scene to be compatible with trains passing by, which locks us into the scale of those parts of the original art that would logically be close to trackside. If the lunchroom is to be close to O scale and the height of the single-story building front (taking the midpoint of the window as a point of reference) is estimated to be about 12 feet, the equivalent width of the scene in the painting works out to about 30 scale feet. As noted in the sidebar illustration, at 7½" in O scale that's compatible with our minimum viewing distance.

To catch the effect of the scene, our viewpoint should be similarly close. Allowing for reasonable nosiness, the front window should be within a foot or so of the aisle. If it's located farther back, the scene may still be interesting, but its perspective will be less angular and the painting's composition — also vital to its

mood-capturing qualities — won't come through nearly as intensely.

Well, in practice what this theoretical stuff tells us is that the 18" width of the intervening yard trackage alongside the Canandaigua Southern's route through downtown Cattaraugus (off-scale to the right in fig. 1) is just too wide; the restaurant will have to be located somewhere left of the East End tower, where only the single main track headed for Dunellen intrudes. At an elevation of 49", this track is well below the 60" to 66" (standing) eye level of most viewers. This suggests that raising the street about 6" (24 scale feet) to the level of a bridge over the track will greatly improve the effectiveness of the scene.

Hopper's restaurant is believed to be based on one — long since gone — at a three-street intersection in New York City's Greenwich Village. Even though I'd never thought of Cattaraugus as populous enough to support an all-night cafe with at least a 12-stool counter, justifying the scene has simply been a matter of envisioning some nearby but off-stage three-shift industry big enough to keep a few hardy souls on the streets at all hours. Extending the "urbanized" scene about 2 feet beyond previous plans does move the next station (Dunellen) that much closer, but adding a couple of overpasses should help restore the *apparent* separation between the two.

PRESERVING THOSE ANGLES

Once the general location has been determined, the process of reconciling the picture with the available real estate can begin. With the Sledgehammer Industrial Park already in business and too lucrative to be shortened appreciably, the right side of the restaurant building is essentially fixed. We already have a row of building backsides that

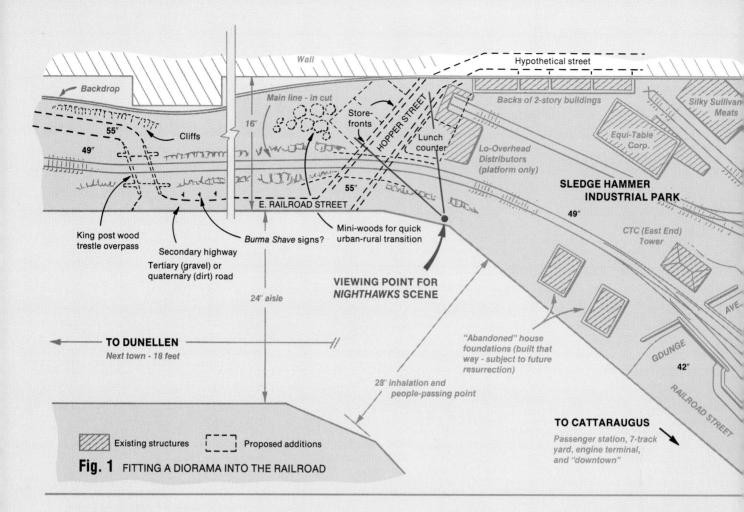

Fig. 1 diagram labels:

Backdrop

Wall

Hypothetical street

Main line - in cut

Store-fronts

HOPPER STREET

Lunch counter

Backs of 2-story buildings

Silky Sullivan Meats

Equi-Table Corp.

55"

Cliffs

16"

49"

Lo-Overhead Distributors (platform only)

SLEDGE HAMMER INDUSTRIAL PARK

55"

E. RAILROAD STREET

49"

CTC (East End) Tower

King post wood trestle overpass

Secondary highway

Tertiary (gravel) or quaternary (dirt) road

Burma Shave signs?

Mini-woods for quick urban-rural transition

VIEWING POINT FOR *NIGHTHAWKS* SCENE

24" aisle

← TO DUNELLEN —

Next town - 18 feet

"Abandoned" house foundations (built that way - subject to future resurrection)

GDUNGE

42"

RAILROAD STREET

28" inhalation and people-passing point

TO CATTARAUGUS

Passenger station, 7-track yard, engine terminal, and "downtown"

Existing structures   Proposed additions

Fig. 1 FITTING A DIORAMA INTO THE RAILROAD

can only be rationalized by the "existence" of a hypothetical street behind the very real wall and backdrop; this we will somehow need to join with the street to the left of the restaurant.

Across the street, those shadowy buildings can be seen end-on and so must be of more than movie-set depth behind the recessed doorways that contribute so much to the mystique of the painting. Another complication is the sidewalk area in the foreground, brightly lit by the overhead lights within the restaurant, whose contrast with the dark building front is also so essential a part of the powerful composition.

"Designing" the buildings to match the scene is a process similar to, though less precise than, the one we use in modeling a piece of rolling stock when only one photograph is available. We start with some element whose size is reasonably well established (here, the 30″ spacing typical for lunch-counter stools will do) and, with due regard for the effects of perspective, deduce all other dimensions from that. See fig. 2. The same process — with the advantage of those precisely known railroad dimensions — is of course applicable in working under the inspiration of a similarly closeup railroad painting or an art photograph such as one of O. Winston Link's classic Norfolk & Western night scenes.

It's probable that the corner of the lunchroom that was the basis of Hopper's

scene matched the angle of intersection of the adjacent streets — possibly as acute as 45 degrees. From a single viewpoint it's impossible to say what the angle is, so we can adjust the angle to preserve those things in the scene that create its mood.

A key aspect of most masterpieces is *ambiguity* — by leaving some things open to different interpretations, the artist gets the viewer involved in coming up with ideas of his own that may go well beyond anything the painter himself had in mind.

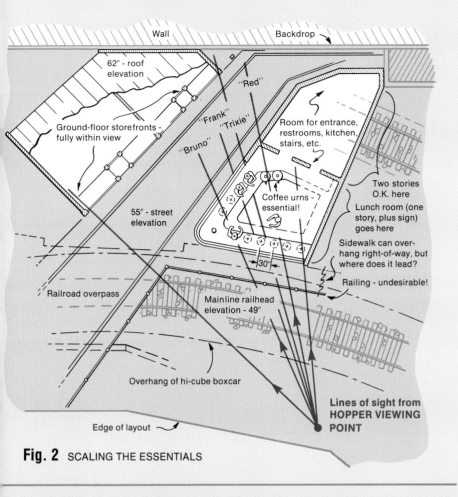

Fig. 2 SCALING THE ESSENTIALS

Labels in figure:
Wall
Backdrop
62" - roof elevation
"Red"
Ground-floor storefronts - fully within view
"Frank"
"Trixie"
"Bruno"
Room for entrance, restrooms, kitchen, stairs, etc.
55" - street elevation
Coffee urns - essential!
Two stories O.K. here
Lunch room (one story, plus sign) goes here
Sidewalk can overhang right-of-way, but where does it lead?
30'
Railing - undesirable!
Railroad overpass
Mainline railhead elevation - 49"
Overhang of hi-cube boxcar
Lines of sight from HOPPER VIEWING POINT
Edge of layout

With positioning central to the scene's meaning, it become essential to maintain the angular lines of sight from a specific viewpoint past Bruno, Frank, Trixie, and Red in the right order and intersecting such background features as the kitchen door and coffee urns in a comparable pattern. By the way, names were given to these four characters to distinguish their identities, positions, and viewing angles while available figures were modified to resemble those in the painting.

BACK THROUGH THE WALL

In the artist's situation, things have to hang together from only one chosen viewpoint. We, on the other hand, have to find room for such other essential auxiliaries as cooking facilities and some way for customers to get into the joint. As the available space works out, it's apparent that if the street is to go somewhere — to the right, behind the flats to the rear, as a first choice — the restaurant building will be too small to accommodate an entrance, a kitchen of even short-order size, and a staircase to a second story. (Yes, we must have a staircase to bring the building up to eye level and hide the nearness of the wall.)

Since there's no room for the street to turn left either, the only practical solution is to extend it through the wall with a mirror. As fig. 3 shows, this introduces some complications — the street must bend to the right enough to block direct, 90-degree reflection and thus prevent the viewer from seeing his own out-of-scale eyeball shining in the background. But it does allow at least an alley-size thoroughfare (we do what we can to help by putting up one-way signs) twisting past a building that can now appear long enough to contain more than just the beanery.

In my case, the workings of the surplus market made it possible to use a front-surface, plate-glass mirror of considerably better quality than ordinarily on hand for such a purpose. This was done at the expense of adapting the scene to its width by making the alley a scale foot or so narrower than might otherwise have been desirable.

The most serious problem in the realistic use of a mirror for such space-expansion is hiding its top edge. I relied on an overhead banner advertising the forthcoming Cattaraugus Firemen's Carnival stretched across the street to do the job. This worked better than adding the meteorologically astounding cotton cloud that modelers sometimes use out of desperation where a bridge would look even worse.

Art historians analyzing the subtleties of *Nighthawks* have made it clear that the positioning of the four figures is as crucial as their individual representations. Some see them as Ernest Hemingway characters only a few minutes away from homicide. Others suggest that a cash register (either the one across the way or another in the restaurant itself, out-of-sight but assumed) is a key target. And still others see the scene more innocently as a simple matter of third-shift isolation.

Far left: The author had to include items in his modeled cafe that don't show in the painting, such as the grill, cash register, pie case, and exit to the rest rooms. **Left:** This view shows how the cafe fits into the overall street scene. Space restrictions meant that only a narrow street was possible, which is why it was made one-way. The street angles into a mirror whose top edge is hidden by the big Firemen's Carnival banner.

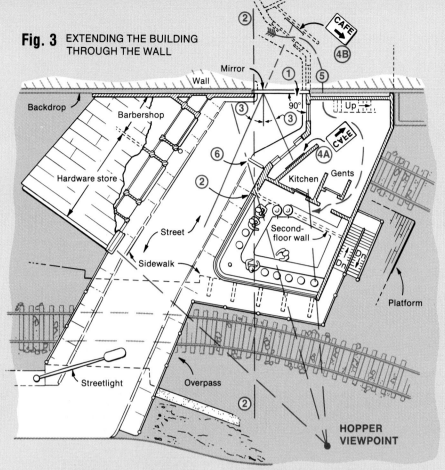

Fig. 3 EXTENDING THE BUILDING THROUGH THE WALL

1. Wall and street surfaces must be precisely perpendicular to mirror or they will appear bent at its surface. Front-surface mirrors will avoid "ghost" images and gap in wall surface. Conceal gap with half-drainpipe "joint" if a rear-surface mirror must be used.

2. Lunch counter window frame (ground floor), and corner of building (second story) cut off direct view of mirror surface (and viewer's eye reflection)!

3. Angle of reflection from mirror surface is always exactly equal to the angle of incidence.

4A. Actual position of entrance door and "cafe" sign (done in reverse; pick lettering easily drawn backwards) is hidden from normal viewing angles.

4B. Apparent (reflected) position of entrance door with "cafe" sign visible on wall inside door.

5. Apparent path for customers from building entrance to lunch counter through area now large enough to contain kitchen, stairs, and other essentials.

6. Neon "EAT" sign, blocked from "Hopper Viewpoint" by second story of building. Back side is blank — so as not to appear reversed if glimpsed in mirror.

Composition

Contriving scenes that go beyond attracting attention

ONE BASIC ELEMENT of all the fine arts (painting, as we've explained, as well as photography and three-dimensional dioramas) is composition. By this we mean the arrangement of what is seen to obtain the best effect on the viewer. To quote one encyclopedia, it's "the balanced arrangement of parts to form one harmonious whole."

Now what artists have sought to depict has changed over the centuries, but human vision has not. That's why our understanding of successful composition has improved. Experience has enabled artists to establish principles of composition that we modelers should be able to use to provide impressive scenes through which we can actually run trains.

Many of the principles simply recognize the field of vision of our eyes. As the drawing illustrates, we see objects clearly within a volume that's roughly oblong in cross section and expands outward towards infinity (or the backdrop) from an inner limit of roughly 7″.

Leaving out the complicating effects of binocular vision, a picture represents what we see by flattening everything beyond onto a foreground "picture plane" perpendicular to the line of sight. Except for portraits, paintings therefore tend to be horizontal in format and of proportions (*e.g.* 16 x 20 feet) more or less corresponding to our field of view.

We want our scenes to be compatible with trains passing by, so foreground elements must also be in or close to their scale. Overlaid on the width and height dimensions at the minimum-focus point in the drawing are their equivalents in terms of our common model railroading scales. What this tells us is that any scene larger than 9 x 12 feet can be comfortably seen as modeled in No. 1 scale (⅜″ = 1′). N scalers will need magnification to focus on any representation of an area smaller than 40 x 53 feet.

[The best starting point for learning how to use mirrors to extend space realistically is an article by John Allen that appeared in the December 1981 MODEL RAILROADER. Please write to Kalmbach Publishing Co. for information on how to obtain back issues, or consult the ad in last month's MR on pages 78 and 79. — *Ed.*]

From this point, the painting's established vanishing points and the elementary principles of perspective make it a matter of developing a plausibly complete set of interior and exterior elements that remain consistent with the part of the scene visible in the painting. These must include (actually or by implication) such essentials as restaurant signs, a building entrance, grill, pie case, and exit to the gents' room, all of which must be located so as to be invisible from the "Hopper" angle.

A major concern is the effect on the scene of the railing alongside the foreground sidewalk — it can be neither omitted nor, in its position, hidden. Luckily, when painted to match its horizontal members virtually disappear against the shadowed wainscot of the restaurant.

Within the space, we have to strain reality here and there, bracketing that sidewalk over the track and then running a stairway down to the loading platform to explain why, for example, Hopper's draftsmanship itself holds up well, with no major discrepancies showing up as remaining elements are fitted into the tableau. Across the way there is room only for "a store and a half," so the second commercial establishment becomes a barbershop.

DECISIONS — BRILLIANT AND OTHERWISE

Since the layout width available at this point was only 16″, I made an early decision — on the basis of limited but generally successful previous experience — to increase the apparent depth by "forcing" the perspective. So I gradually narrowed the street and sidewalks toward the rear.

I also decided to tailor the already out-of-square shape of the buildings a bit, recognizing that the degree of this cheating in the horizontal plane would be limited by the fact that such vertical dimensions as window heights couldn't be similarly fudged. The array of available Grandt Line window castings doesn't include foreshortened or lozenge-shaped versions, and I'm not enough of a masochist to roll my own unnecessarily.

This turned out to be one of those "brilliant" ideas — among plenty of others throughout my modeling career —

These figures don't mean that scenes smaller than indicated can't be looked at and enjoyed — the fact that you'll either see a larger area (the size of a 4-story apartment house in N, for example) or must resort to magnification to concentrate on anything more compact simply means that the perspective of any such scene under conditions where it's seen clearly must correspond to a more distant prototype viewpoint.

In other words, it doesn't make a lot of sense to superdetail in the smaller scales. Instead, apply that effort to making sure that the overall proportions of structures and rolling stock appear correct. Details should be added only in those areas located close enough to viewers to be seen and fully appreciated.

What about the far end of the scene? How do we fare if we seek to re-create the more "train-size" scenes favored by our railroad artists? Since for most of us the locomotive is the thing, the majority of such views are some species of the "¾ wedge" — they feature the head end, yet still include much or most of the whole consist of a full-length train. As you know from trying to buy frames to fit, they logically favor the proportions of their subject by being considerably more oblong than standard.

For a broadside view, it's often a matter of how far back you can stand. That, in turn, is largely a function of aisle width and arm length. So, the broadside-view drawing shows how much of a train we can see if it's located toward the rear of a scene hemmed in by such considerations — a field of view about 4 feet wide. Horizontally, you can think of this in terms of the approximate number of 40-foot freight cars within sight. As you'd expect, the smaller scales have the edge, though stepping back to experience the grandeur of the scene makes it impossible to notice the fine detail it took so long to build into the models.

Generally speaking, we're going to look at the trains at that ¾-wedge angle, which improves the situation. However, even in the smallest scales the trains we can see from end to end will tend to remain of model rather than full mainline length.

As your field of view gets wider, it also gets higher — almost 3 feet in our back-of-the-aisle case, and much higher than that if you turn to look along the scene. In terms of railroad or urban structures, this is good; Superman probably

CLOSEUP RELATIONSHIPS

4" wide

60°

No. 1 = 12 ft.
O = 16 ft.
S = 21 ft.
HO = 29 ft.
N = 53 ft.
Z = 73 ft.

7" closest focus

45°

No. 1 = 9 ft.
O = 12 ft.
S = 16 ft.
HO = 22 ft.
N = 40 ft.
Z = 55 ft.

3" high

No scale

FIELD OF VISION

BROADSIDE VIEW — SEEN FROM ABOVE

60°

No. 1 = 3 cars
O = 4 cars
S = 6 cars
HO = 8 cars
N = 15 cars
Z = 20 cars
(40' cars)

24" aisle — Arm's length

wouldn't consider the 12-story building our eyesight can encompass in O scale particularly insulting, and Z scalers could impress us with a full-scale Washington Monument!

In double-deck layouts and in the larger scales, however, we may run into another problem: This extended field of view may weaken the scene by bringing such extraneous things as the upper deck, top of the backdrop, or ceiling itself within sight. A general remedy is suggested by the theater, in which the darkened face of the proscenium arch — like a properly located light valance — effectively chops the unwanted top from our consciousness.

A MATTER OF VIEWPOINT

Beyond these vision-related matters of foreground scale and overall proportion, other important principles of composition concentrate on guiding the viewer's attention. Such schemes as shadows, framing elements in the foreground, and intersecting angles turn a wayward gaze approaching the margin back toward the centers of interest — the fine-arts equivalent of retaining awareness of a precisely ballasted main line by introducing some shrubbery as the edge of the layout is approached.

Guides at historic mansions and state capitols (art gallery docents are usually somewhat better informed) are wont to claim remarkable properties for large portraits encountered in their tours. They're quick to note, "See how the painter has made the eyes follow you as

you move around." Big deal — it would be remarkable if it could be any other way! Since a painting can represent things only as seen from *a* single point, eyes once so aimed have no choice but to chase the spectator throughout the practical limits of viewing angle.

That does make things considerably simpler for the artist than for those of us working in the solid, but we can often improve the effectiveness of our modeling by planning scenes so they must be seen from the intended direction. Our creations must still hold together and make sense when looked at from a range of viewpoints, but narrowing that range can hide the more unrealistically distorted views.

Our big advantage is the so-called magnet effect of the moving trains that will remain the centerpiece of our scenes, powerful enough to divert attention from all sorts of defects and deficiencies. Since they must remain parts of the operating railroad, we aren't going to put frames around our stationary scenes. However, if they're intriguing enough they can similarly center the viewer's interest and suppress awareness of things that are too far to left or right to be seen without distortion.

In the end, that is our incentive for learning from — or even trying to "copy" in three dimensions — those artistic compositions recognized as masterpieces. They have demonstrated their ability to go beyond merely capturing viewers' interest to affecting their mood. Maybe we can do something like that too! ⌂

---

that have turned out to be far more laborious (as well as less impressive) than expected. The primary problem with forced perspective applied to buildings is that it's a lot more trouble to plan and assemble an out-of-square structure that looks convincing than it is to build and "plant" one that's properly rectangular. It did turn out that the apparent depth of the building across the street from the

restaurant *could* be stretched by subtly decreasing the spacing between its upstairs windows as they "recede" toward the rear of the scene.

NO DETAIL HOUND, FORTUNATELY!

No impressionist, Hopper typically outlined all objects as seen in clear air, while at the same time using highlights and shadows to intensify their solidity and

character. Perhaps to further the feeling of loneliness so characteristic of his more notable pictures, and in marked contrast to the work of some other contemporary realists, there is little or no clutter in his scenes, urban or rural.

Within the present state of the art of our modeling, that clear air is a big help. Clutter we could obviously handle — to the point of gross overkill —

The sidewalk in front of the cafe extends over the Canandaigua Southern's main line here at Cattaraugus, where an Erie Lackawanna NW2 switcher is pushing some passenger cars to the yard.

but it's nice not to have to. As sparse as Hopper's detailing may initially seem, the challenge of re-creating each and every item remains formidable as the scene takes shape in three dimensions.

The mechanics of miniaturization also throw us some curves, even in O scale. For example, until finally glued to the countertop, salt and pepper shakers (whittled from plastic and tipped with a dip in aluminum paint) are amazingly vulnerable to disappearance with a single careless breath. Oh well, the first ones weren't really good enough anyway!

LIGHT AND SHADOW

Lighting is the name of the game, and a challenge it is despite the fortunate fact that in this case it's all indirect and we have no need to limit ourselves to strictly scale lights. The importance of shadow lines to the composition means that the *position* of these unseen light sources is critical. We can approximate

this with oversize bulbs by raising the flat roof behind the Phillies billboard to accommodate enough of them (four in my version) to approach the relatively even, brilliant illumination of the restaurant interior in its contrast with the dim menace of the surrounding scene.

That brings up an irksome principle I've found almost universally applicable in night scenes — realism is not nearly so much a matter of putting the light where you want it as it is of keeping it from shining where it shouldn't! Beyond a certain point (which of course you can find only in retrospect!) it's going to be more efficient to stop designing and start experimenting.

So I tried a one-piece window of clear and rigid .040″ acrylic hot-formed to match the corner curve of Hopper's art deco restaurant. It nicely reproduces the faint reflections he used to subtly separate indoors from out. Unfortunately, we find that the light yellow restaurant

walls reflect overpoweringly in the darkened windows across the street. Since you can't tell from the painting what color the right-hand wall actually is, we can alleviate some of the problem by painting it dark green. The back wall does show, so it must stay yellow.

This example shows that, within the limits of our perspective and proportions, we simply will not be able to duplicate the painting precisely. Perhaps the angles were different in the "prototype," or Hopper used painter's license to strengthen his composition. Regardless, we'll just hope that the discrepancy won't seriously weaken the overall scene.

Color balance can also be a problem. Although lighting within the lift-out buildings is powered via pigtails plugged into jacks mounted within their foundations, prudence dictates minimizing bulb replacement by operating well below nominal voltage. At some cost in brightness, the resulting yellowish cast can be partially compensated by painting any reflecting surfaces a pale blue.

What effect does this have? We're fortunate that the impact seems minimal. Visually, our eyes are forgiving — though some of Hopper's lonely mood may still be lost in the less chilling glow. Photographically, of course, both filters and color compensation in processing are available to those of us who aren't completely honest.

LESSONS?

Judging from experience, as soon as the scene takes shape its source is recognizable to anyone who is even vaguely acquainted with *Nighthawks*. Whether we've captured the mood of Hopper's painting is something you'll have to judge from the pictures.

Modeling lessons? Perhaps because I look for excuses to be lazy, I'm even more convinced that devoting time and attention to light and shadow will enable us to spend less time on detailing — exactly as Hopper did — those essentials that define the mood of a scene. How do you find out what is essential and what isn't? I suppose the only answer is doing as much detailing as possible in places and realizing that those things that consume the most time generally turn out to have little effect. Such a philosophy makes acceptable those frequent pauses for contemplating results that I find are inevitable anyway.

A single shot is nothing much. Are there other pictures it might be fun to "copy?" Since I naturally started out with a favorite, maybe there are no others that I would find *fully* as interesting. But I know that Hopper also painted some challenging rural scenes, and I suspect that among the hundreds of works done by realists in the last 150 years, or even before the railroad's birth, there are bound to be a number of other inspiring scenes. And then there are all those railroad-artist paintings, not to mention photos! So I think I'm just beginning to explore what fine art has to offer model railroading. ⚙

Ratio 1:48 O scale

Today's outdoor advertising

CHRYSLER-Plymouth and Heinz USA graciously provided us with samples of their advertising so we could help you add contemporary billboards to your model railroads. Chrysler-Plymouth's artwork is actual outdoor advertising, while Heinz developed the "Heinz 57 Sauce" billboard for our use. Our thanks to both firms for their help. ✿

Ratio 1:64 S scale

Ratio 1:160 N scale

Ratio 1:87 HO scale

Ratio 1:48 O scale

Ratio 1:48 O scale

Billboards from the past

OUR THANKS to the Institute of Ourdoor Advertising for allowing us to reprint these examples of billboards, which come from their publication *The Big Outdoor*. Unfortunately, neither ad can be dated precisely. We know they come from the pre-World War II years, but can't be certain of when. Any help readers can provide will be appreciated. ⬦

Ratio 1:64 S scale

Ratio 1:160 N scale

Ratio 1:87 HO scale

Ratio 1:48 O scale

Smokey the Bear posters

SMOKEY the Bear began fighting forest fires in 1944. Perhaps no other poster campaign has been so extensive or so successful: for 40 years Smokey literally has been a household name. These posters decorating the station platforms, board fences, and building walls on your layout will add a familiar and realistic touch. ✿

Smokey Bear and fire prevention posters used by permission of the USDA Forest Service.

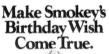

48-star flags

IN 1912 two stars were added to the American flag when Arizona and New Mexico became the 47th and 48th states. Old Glory didn't change until 1959, when Alaska and Hawaii joined the Union, so these flags are appropriate for a model railroad layout set anytime in that 47-year period. In the future we'll provide 50-star flags for post-1959 modelers. Your flags will look best if attached to a line, rather than wrapped directly around the pole. Most flagpoles used by small businesses and government institutions are 18 feet high. ✿

18'-0" standard

Fine thread or wire

Standard flag proportion is 3 x 5 units

Not to scale

Tubing or wire flagpole

S SCALE
Ratio 1:64

HO SCALE
Ratio 1:87

O SCALE
Ratio 1:48

N SCALE   Ratio 1:160

50-star flags

THE 50th star was officially added to the American flag on July 4, 1960, when a 50-star flag was first raised above Independence Hall in Philadelphia. That flag was then presented for safekeeping to Senator Hiram Fong, representing the 50th state, Hawaii. (The 49th star, Alaska's, had been added the previous Fourth of July.) The flags here are for use with each of the major modeling scales, but there's no reason why several sizes couldn't be used on a layout. An HO modeler, for example, might use an S scale flag atop a large industry or an N scale flag on the rear of a power boat. Modelers with layouts set before 1960 will find 48-star flags in last year's July issue. ○

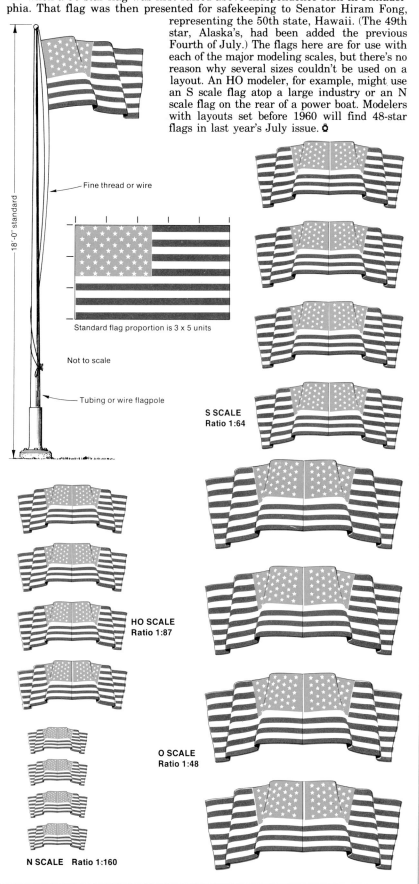

18'-0" standard

Fine thread or wire

Standard flag proportion is 3 x 5 units

Not to scale

Tubing or wire flagpole

S SCALE
Ratio 1:64

HO SCALE
Ratio 1:87

O SCALE
Ratio 1:48

N SCALE   Ratio 1:160

Index